AIR ADVENTURES

Landmarks in the True Story of Flight

Graeme Cook

Other books by the same author

Wings of Glory	(Hart Davis)
None But the Valiant	(Hart Davis)
Commandos In Action	(Hart Davis, MacGibbon)
Spotlight on Aircraft	(Hamlyn)

AIR ADVENTURES

Landmarks in the True Story of Flight

Graeme Cook

ST. MARTIN'S PRESS · NEW YORK

Contents

To Gary, my son

Acknowledgements

I should like to express my thanks to the Curator and staff of the Royal Air Force Museum, Hendon, whose unparalleled display of historic and modern aircraft provided me with close-up views of many of the aeroplanes featured in this book. My thanks are also due to the Director and staff of the Imperial War Museum, London, for their invaluable help in my research.

For the extracts reproduced from radio talks by the then Squadron Leaders Hamlyn and Semple my thanks are due to the British Broadcasting Corporation and to the officers concerned.

Should the reader wish to delve deeper into any of the subjects or events related here, I can wholeheartedly recommend the following books:-

The Dam Busters, Paul Brickhill (Evans Bros., 1951)

Reach for The Sky, Paul Brickhill (Collins, 1954)

The Worlds Greatest Air Mysteries, Michael Hardwick (Odhams, 1970)

The Battle of Britain, Edward Bishop (Allen & Unwin, 1960)

Early Aviation, Sir Robert Saundby (Macdonald, 1971)

Famous Fighters of the Second World War (series) William Green (Macdonald)

Famous Bombers of the Second World War (series) William Green (Macdonald)

Warplanes of the First World War (series) J.M. Bruce (Macdonald)

Warplanes of the Second World War (series) William Green (Macdonald)

Kitty Hawk to Concorde, H.F. King & J.W.R. Taylor (Jane's, 1970)

Fighter Squadrons of the R.A.F., John Rawlings (Macdonald, 1969)

Bomber Squadrons of the R.A.F., Philip Moyes (Macdonald, 1964)

Luftwaffe, Alfred Price (Macdonald, 1970)
German Secret Weapons, Brian Ford (Macdonald, 1970)
Great Air Stories (Collins, 1970)
Richthofen, William E. Burrows (Hart-Davis, 1970)
Six Great Aviators, John Pudney (Hamish Hamilton, 1955)
The Royal Flying Corps: A History, Geoffrey Norris (Muller, 1965)
The Great Air War, Aaron Norman (Macmillan, 1968)
Aces High, Shores & Williams (Neville Spearman, 1966)
Men of Glory, Macdonald Hastings (Hulton, 1958)
More Men of Glory, Macdonald Hastings (Hulton, 1959)
History of the First World War, Sir Basil Liddell-Hart (Cassell, 1970) History of the Second World War, Sir Basil Liddell-Hart (Cassell, 1970)
Mannock V.C., Frederick Oughton (Neville Spearman, 1966)
Full Circle, J.E. Johnson (Chatto & Windus, 1964)

Also the following magazine and partwork publications:-
Purnell's History of the First World War
Purnell's History of the Second World War
Flight International

Introduction

Few young men can fail to be stirred by the excitement conjured up in the mind by the story of flight and flying. Since man first took to the air in a powered aeroplane, flying has provided all the ingredients of adventure, whether in peace or in war.

Perhaps the most staggering feature of the story of the aeroplane is its remarkably fast development. This is due in no small measure to the two World Wars which have been fought in this century. It is ironic to consider that, had it not been for those two terrible conflicts, the aeroplane might still have been in its infancy. Instead of marvelling as we do at the great strides man has made into outer space, we might today have been witnessing only the first transatlantic flight or the coming of the first jet-powered aircraft. Spurred on by the urgent need for aircraft superior to those of their enemies, the major nations of the world spent billions of pounds on developing the aeroplane as a fighting weapon. Then, from the military aircraft used in wartime, were developed the passenger and transport aircraft of peacetime. Had it not been for those wars, such aircraft as Concorde and the Boeing 747 Jumbo jet might still have been merely pipe-dreams.

But no matter what technological advances had been made, the aeroplane would still have been mere useless scrap-metal without a man to fly it, a navigator to guide it over the continents and oceans of the world and the other vital crewmen needed to keep it in the air. This book is not intended to be just a series of chapters which map the development of the aeroplane but more importantly, the story of the men who flew them in peace and in war.

Some of the great names in pioneering flight are contained in this volume....the Wright brothers, Alcock and Brown, Charles Lindbergh and Kingsford-Smith. They were the leaders in the early pioneering days. But the men who went to war in aeroplanes were in their own way pioneers as well, expanding the limits of the possible under the stresses of combat. Pilots like Ball, Richthofen, Gibson, Bader, as well as the backroom scientists like Barnes Wallis who developed and designed aeroplanes and their weapon systems – all played their vital part. Their stories are here. Read on....

1
First Hops

In December 1903, on a lonely wind-swept beach known by the ominous name of Kill Devil Hill, at Kitty Hawk, in North Carolina, U.S.A., two American bicycle mechanics, Wilbur and Orville Wright, made what is now considered to be man's most significant contribution to flight. They succeeded, where many others had failed, in making the first-ever sustained, controlled flight in a heavier-than-air machine under its own power.

When we look back over the intervening seventy years, it is hard to believe that that important 'first hop' was regarded by most of the Wrights' fellow Americans as something of a fluke, attained by a pair of crack-pot inventors. Indeed this epic flight received virtually no publicity in the United States and certainly no acclaim from the nation's scientists. Perhaps this was because many American scientists had claimed that it was *impossible* for men to fly in a heavier-than-air craft, and they were reluctant to admit that they had been proved wrong.

1

This achievement of the Wrights had not come easily or quickly. In fact, it had taken them some three years of hard work carried out in the face of sceptical comments from a number of eminent American scientists. To these men they seemed no more than cranks who might best be left alone to potter with their crazy ideas and models.

It was in 1900 that the Wright brothers, who hailed from Drayton, Ohio, first seriously turned their attentions to the possibility of powered flight. Both of them had been devotees of the German glider designer Otto Lilienthal who had made a series of successful flights in his own gliders. The German was an ornithologist of some distinction in his home country and while studying birds very closely had thought of the idea of applying the aerodynamic principles of bird flight to the design of an aircraft which could carry a man. Lilienthal eventually built his first glider and followed it with many more, making a great number of successful flights.

Lilienthal tended to concentrate his efforts on perfecting his gliders rather than on the possibility of installing a power plant in them. Perhaps his greatest contributions to aviation were the detailed and highly accurate notes he made on his designs and the way his gliders performed in flight, the problems he encountered and the successes he achieved. Lilienthal was eventually killed in 1896 when the glider he was flying crashed, but the legacy he left in the form of these notes and scientific papers was to prove invaluable. The Wright brothers studied the material with great care.

In 1899, the brothers built a biplane kite with a wing span of five feet to test the use of warping wings. Their experiments proved successful and there evolved from their design a glider with a wing span of seventeen feet in which both of them flew. These early glider flights were merely stepping stones in their ambition to achieve powered flight and while they continued to experiment with their glider, they also worked on developing a light-weight internal combustion engine which they hoped they could ultimately install in one of their aircraft.

Not all their gliders had proved successful, so when they now built yet another they decided to rely upon the results of their own investigations rather than the findings of Lilienthal. This proved to be the turning point. They left nothing to chance. They even built a special wind tunnel in which they studied a whole variety of aerofoil sections and how these reacted to wind conditions and speeds. Then in 1903, with their investigations complete, they built the Wright *Flyer*.

The *Flyer*, which looked just like an enormous kite with a forty-foot wing span, was built of wood and cheesecloth. It did not appear to be a particularly robust construction, considering it had to carry the engine, situated in the middle of the lower biplane wing, and a pilot, who had to lie in the prone position and operate the controls. It had no undercarriage wheels as we know them but was designed to run on a trolley which in turn ran on a rail for the take-off. Instead of pulling the aircraft through the air, as in modern propeller-driven aircraft, the propellers of the *Flyer* were situated aft of the wings and were of the 'pusher' type. In its complete form the *Flyer* resembled a pair of long wings with a flimsy tail jutting out behind and with a secondary set of smaller wings fixed on wooden poles in front. Nothing could have looked less likely to take to the air without collapsing in a tangled heap on to the ground – yet it did....

The first attempt came on the 14th of December 1903, when, with Wilbur at the controls, the engine roared into life and the *Flyer* staggered along its rail. The attempt was, however, a failure and that time the *Flyer* did not succeed in getting off the ground. Then, four days later, on the 17th, Orville Wright took up his position, lying flat on the cushioned bench amidships on the *Flyer*. Once more the engine burst into life and the propellers spun. Slowly at first, then gradually gaining speed, the *Flyer* nosed along the rail with Wilbur beside it. Faster and faster it went until, at last, much to the amazement of a group of onlookers nearby, it lifted into the air. Astounded, they stood and watched as the aircraft flew on for all of twelve seconds before gently touching down. It had covered no less than 120 feet, and the Wrights had proved their point, achieving what man had, till then, only dreamed of.

Spurred on by their success, the brothers made three more flights and achieved the staggering distance of 852 feet with a flight lasting fifty-nine seconds. Orville and Wilbur were elated beyond belief but alas the importance of their tremendous achievement was utterly lost on the American public.

But though they had failed to make any impact on their own people, they certainly made a deep impression upon the French who instantly appreciated the significance of their achievement. France had been the birth-place of the balloon and aviation was a popular activity in that country. French aeroplane designers who had hitherto failed to achieve what the Wrights had done, lost no time in inviting them to France so that they too could see the amazing machine which had actually flown. These men were quick to spot where their own designs had gone wrong. Modifying their machines in the light of the knowledge they had gleaned from the Wrights, they were soon achieving even more spectacular successes.

Stronger machines were built, capable of better performances, longer flights and higher altitudes. With engines better adapted to continuous high-speed running, aeroplanes became more reliable and some designers actually began to think of the comfort of the pilot by incorporating cockpits. In the space of just a few years the aeroplane made a truly dramatic change, yet it was still regarded by most people as a plaything, something to amuse the rich when they tired of other amusements.

It was not until 1909 that the true potential of the aeroplane was realised by the world. In that year, a Frenchman, Jean Louis Blériot performed a feat that really caught the public imagination. For some time he had been working on aircraft designs of his own and had suffered many accidents as a result of his attempts to fly. But nothing daunted him – that is until he caught sight of the Wright *Flyer*. That American aircraft impressed him so much that, scrapping all his previous designs, he set out to re-think his whole designing concept. The result emerged from his workshop as the Blériot X1, a high-wing wire-braced monoplane powered by an Anzani 3-cylinder air-cooled engine. On this machine only the wings and tail unit were covered with fabric, the rest being left open to the elements.

At 4.41 a.m., on the 25th of July 1909, Louis Blériot took off in the Blériot X1 from Les Baraques, near Calais, and headed out over the English Channel. He had no compass and had to rely on pure guesswork to guide him but at 5.17 a.m. he landed in Northfall Meadow, near Dover Castle, England, to become the first man ever to fly across the English Channel in a heavier-than-air craft. The Channel was a visible barrier; its conquest a spectacular feat. The aeroplane was at last seen to have possibilities as a genuinely new form of transport.

More highly-sophisticated machines were soon developed and, particularly in France, people thronged from far and wide to watch displays given by daring pilots like Louis Blériot and Henri Farman. It was Blériot who achieved the distinction of becoming the first man ever to loop-the-loop in an aeroplane. No longer was the flying machine restricted to straight and level flight; it could now bank, turn, dive steeply and climb with some degree of rapidity. This was something never seen before, a machine at home in three dimensions, fast, exhilarating, *free*.

With the speedy development of the aeroplane, a few far-sighted men began to consider its use as an instrument of war. Trouble was brewing in Europe and war seemed near. But how could an aeroplane be used in battle? Too flimsy to be capable of carrying any offensive weapon to damage an enemy, aeroplanes might, however, be used for observation purposes. Spying out the lie of the land and spotting enemy gun emplacements and troop movements, they could then pass the information back to the military commanders.

When war eventually came in August 1914, most military men discounted the aeroplane as an offensive weapon. The generals of the day placed greater faith in the cavalry charge to win their battles than in the new-fangled flying machine. Nevertheless steps had been taken by the major nations to build up air forces of a sort, however small. At that time the newly-founded British Royal Flying Corps had a mere handful of unarmed machines consisting of Bleriots, B.E.2s, Avros and Farmans.

Soon after the outbreak of war, the ill-equipped R.F.C. sent thirty-seven aircraft, almost its total strength, over to France with the British Expeditionary Force. Their function was to act as observers and, being part of the army, they came under the immediate control of the military commanders, who were free to use them as they thought fit.

The German Air Service acted likewise, sending their planes over the Allied lines to spy on the British and French armies. In those early days it was quite a common occurrence for Allied and German aeroplanes to fly past each other as they went on their missions and exchange greetings with a friendly wave. After all, neither pilot could do the other any harm. But the comparative freedom from attack which airmen enjoyed, in the air above the battlegrounds was soon to be brought abruptly to an end.

For one day it occurred to an Allied pilot that he ought not to allow the Germans to come blithely flying over his ground to see what the troops on his side were doing. Armed with this information they would fly home to spread the news amongst the artillery gunners who would in turn send a devastating barrage of fire down upon the Allied troops in the trenches. Since the results of these bombardments were horrific in the extreme and thousands of men were losing their lives daily as a result of the well aimed and directed fire, this young pilot thought that he would do something to stop it. He decided to take along with him his sporting rifle which he had brought from England.

He took off from his base with the rifle nestling in the cockpit beside him, fully loaded. Gaining height he flew on over the German lines until at last he spotted a German plane flying towards him en route for the British lines. As the two aircraft drew closer to each other, the German raised his arm to wave a friendly 'good morning'. But as he did so, the British pilot 'drew' his rifle, levelled it, took aim and fired at the enemy plane as it flashed past. The German could hardly believe his ears as the bullets whined past his aircraft. Though the British pilot had missed by a considerable distance the German was so taken aback by what had happened that he threw his aircraft into a steep turn and headed at full speed for home.

This brief encounter set the pilots of both sides thinking. Soon more and more of them were arming themselves with a weird assortment of weapons to use against their enemies. Some carried rifles, while others 'packed' shotguns and revolvers. Few of them ever actually succeeded in *hitting* an enemy aircraft, let alone doing it any serious damage. More often the damage was actually sustained by the man firing the weapon. Time and again, aircraft returned to base with their wings, tails and fuselage peppered with holes – not from enemy bullets but from their own!

Some of the more inventive pilots, particularly the French, set their minds to discovering what other types of weapons they could use and gradually built up a formidable arsenal of 'hardware'. Building bricks became standard equipment with which the pilots tried to 'bomb' their opponents, hoping to smash a wing or damage some vital part of the fuselage. But bricks were far from aerodynamically sound and seldom fell with any accuracy. Few, if any, hit the enemy aircraft at which they were aimed. Usually they succeeded only in slowing down the aircraft which carried them, by their added weight.

Other pilots took along darts – like the ones thrown at dart boards but very much larger and with fearsome points. But like the brick-throwing these aerial darts matches proved unsuccessful. Next the cunning aviators went on to arm themselves with great lengths of rope at the end of which they tied their bricks. The idea was to fly close above an enemy in the hope that his propeller would be fouled by the rope. But the rope-trick did not work either.

Puzzled as to how to attack other aircraft, one pilot decided to ignore them and turned his attentions to the German troops on the ground. He loaded up his cockpit with hand-grenades and when over the enemy lines dived low and tossed a few into the trenches. It gave him the greatest satisfaction to see them exploding on target but he was less happy when the troops opened up at him with rifle-fire peppering the vulnerable underparts of his aircraft with bullets. Protective armour plating had not then been intro-duced, but after this pilot's harrowing experience it was hastily built into all aircraft.

In spite of their initial set-backs, these cavaliers of the sky remained undaunted and indeed became even more deter-mined to 'have a crack' at the enemy by whatever means they could manage.

On the 25th of August, 1914, a flight of three R.F.C. aircraft, led by Lieutenant Harvey Kelly, took off on a patrol behind enemy lines. Their job was a routine one, to observe the enemy positions and movements and report back to headquarters. They had not been in the air long when Kelly spotted a lone German aircraft far below them heading for the British lines.

'Here's my chance,' Harvey Kelly thought and he signalled to his wingmen that he was going down.

Pushing forward his control column he sent the aircraft into a near-vertical dive, closely followed by his other two aircraft. Down they plunged with the ground racing up towards them. The screech of their engines reached the ears of the German pilot who tried to escape the oncoming aircraft which seemed all set to ram him. He put his aircraft into a dive, but he had been flying quite low and soon the ground became dangerously close. There seemed to be no means of escape from the crazy Englishmen.

'They must be mad,' he thought. 'If they hit me we'll all be killed.'

By then he was barely a couple of hundred feet from the ground and certain of disaster unless he acted fast. There was only one thing to do. Levelling off a scant few feet from the ground, he chose a field not far off and set the aircraft down on it, slithering to a halt near a dense wood.

Harvey Kelly looked on amazed as he, too, levelled off. The terrified German pilot was leaping out of his cockpit and dashing towards the wood, leaving his aircraft. Kelly was not going to miss such a chance. Wheeling round he landed alongside the stationary German plane. Then he too jumped out of his cockpit, armed only with a box of matches. Quickly he ran to the enemy machine, lit a match, and set fire to it. Then fearing that the German might be armed with some more substantial weapon and decide to take a few pot-shots at him he jumped into his aircraft, took off and returned to base to the resounding cheers of his fellow pilots. Harvey Kelly had got the Royal Flying Corps' first 'kill' – and not a single shot had been fired!

When we look back on these early days of flying and aerial combat we tend to regard them as something comical but it must never be forgotten that these men were the poineers, airmen who risked their lives by even *taking off* in an aeroplane at a time when it was not uncommon for aircraft simply to fold up in the air for no apparent reason. The aeroplane itself was in its infancy then and so indeed was aerial warfare, but the day of the great fighter aces like Ball, Richthofen and Mannock was dawning. With them would come the real fighter aircraft, the Sopwiths, Fokkers and Albatroses, which were to write history in the sky. The battle over Europe was just beginning......

2
Albert Ball, VC

Captain Albert Ball's eyes scanned the clear blue sky over the battle-torn French country-side one day in 1917 as he nursed his Nieuport Scout fighter through the air. He was looking for the enemy; eager for action.

Below Ball lay mile upon mile of land scarred by trenches and pock-marked by thousands of shell-holes where the bloodiest battle of all history was raging. Already hundreds of thousands of men had died in that inferno. The country-side for as far as he could see had taken on an almost lunar appearance, pitted with vast craters gouged out of the ground by the shells of both sides raining down upon it. That was the vista unfolded before Ball. But he had seen all this before many times and he had to clear his mind of that war raging beneath him. He had his own war to wage – in the air, where his adversaries of the German Air Service lurked in their fighters ready to pounce in their dozens upon the lone fighter.

Ball swung his Scout round in a tight turn, his eyes

sweeping the sky above and below him as he did so. Then he spotted them – two German Albatros fighters making their way back to their lines after a foray into British territory. The Englishman cocked his guns then pushed the Scout forward into a steep dive and plunged down on the two Germans. They did not spot him until the sound of his racing engine reached their ears, then they broke formation.

Ball picked out one of them and closed for the kill with his guns blazing. The rattle of machine-gun fire shook the Scout as bullets ripped and tore into the Albatros, smashing through struts and puncturing the canvas covering. The Scout closed on the German with guns still chattering, but try as he might Ball could not gain the advantage and deliver the fatal blow that would send the Albatros hurtling down. Luck was with the German for as Ball's bullets traced a line of holes along the fuselage towards his cockpit, the Scout's guns suddenly fell silent. Ball had run out of ammunition.

The damaged German plane lurched as the German pilot fought to control it. Realising what had happened he turned for home. The other Albatros was already well on its way back to base. But Ball was not a man to give up as easily as that. He stayed on the tail of the limping German and pulled his .38 revolver from its holster then, steadying the Scout with his left hand on the control column, he fired six rounds from it at the fleeing aircraft. But in the turbulent air, with his plane bucking and dipping his aim was not true and the German flew on untouched. Ball still would not give up and followed the two Albatroses back to their own airfield deep in the heart of enemy territory watching frustratedly as they landed safely while he circled high above.

Wheeling round over the German airfield while the gunners below took pot-shots at him, he pulled a note-pad and pencil from a pocket in his flying suit and hurriedly scribbled a message on it. It was a challenge to the two Albatroses to do battle with him again at dawn the following day! Diving low over the airfield he dropped the note, watched with a wry smile as it fluttered down, then lifted the Scout's nose in a climb. Glancing back he watched as several tiny figures raced to where it had landed. They had got the challenge, he thought, but would they take him up on it?

The following morning, as the first light of dawn crept over the airfield, Ball clambered into the cockpit of his

Nieuport and strapped himself in. Soon the engine burst into life breaking the stillness of the early morning. He eased open the throttle and the Scout trundled forward, rocking over the uneven ground, then he swung into wind and gave the frail plane full power. The Scout shook as it gathered speed then the tail lifted and Ball eased back on the joystick. The aircraft was free of the ground and climbing into the cold air.

As he gained height Ball set course for the position where, the day before, he had done battle with the Albatroses. As he neared the area he caught sight of his two adversaries, lying in wait. They had accepted the challenge.

Ball, a believer in bold tactics, wasted no time. Jabbing forward his throttle he charged in to the attack, selecting the nearer of the two Germans as his first target. With his finger poised over the trigger of his twin machine-guns, Ball's intent eyes never left the Albatros as it grew larger in his gunsight. He could sense that the German was nervous and would break away as the charging Scout approached. He was a sitting duck – an easy target. Yet, was he *too* easy. There was something unnatural about these tactics. The German was not taking evasive action, and he must have seen Ball coming in. Before Ball realised what was happening, it was too late. His finger was curled round the trigger, squeezing on the first pressure when it happened....

Suddenly a hail of bullets zipped past his aircraft from above. Ball broke off the attack and pulled hard back on his control column, sending the Scout careering skywards. He had been lured into a trap. What a fool he had been, he thought, to fall into an obvious ambush like this. There above him and plummeting down towards him with guns blazing were three other Albatroses. His adversaries had brought along some extra support. The age of chivalry was over, Ball thought. The Germans must have decided that he was too great a prize to lose through any scruples of honour.

Ball was in a tight spot. The odds were five to one against him getting out of the fight alive. To any other pilot such odds would have meant certain death. But Ball did not lose his head. Deciding that the best form of defence was attack, he turned on the Germans, firing at them whenever the opportunity presented itself. But the Germans had obviously worked out in advance just how they would handle him. While three of them lurked behind him, cutting off his line of retreat, the other two 'waved the red rag', presenting themselves as easy targets then dashing out of range before he could fire, and all the while luring him deeper into German territory. But Ball was no mean tactician and the Germans' tactics soon became obvious to him. Unfortunately, just as he realised what they were up to he ran out of ammunition once more. Now his situation was more perilous then ever. He was at their mercy and they knew it. In a matter of seconds they would close in for the kill.

Now the two Germans he had been chasing turned on him to deal the final blow. Both of them bored in with guns rattling a cone of bullets at the Scout and almost instantly the Nieuport fell away into a steep spin tumbling out of control towards the ground. The three Albatroses which had watched the 'kill' left the scene to return to base, satisfied that the great British ace had finally met his doom.

Meanwhile, Ball's aircraft corkscrewed towards the ground with the two Albatroses following it down. The German pilots were determined to see the end of the Englishman who had dared to challenge them to a duel. They watched intently as the Scout hurtled closer and closer to the ground. Then, with only a few hundred feet to spare, the Scout pulled out of the spin and shakily levelled out. Skipping over some trees the British plane nosed in towards a field, bumped down onto the ground, swerving crazily, then finally came to a halt.

The Germans watched, fascinated, realising that Ball could only have been seriously wounded. One German signalled to the other to land in the field and they both put their aircraft down near to where the Scout had halted. They jumped from their aircraft and could see Ball's figure slumped over the controls in his cockpit. His engine was still ticking over as the Germans neared the plane. Then they stopped dead in their tracks as the pilot suddenly came to life, sitting up in the cockpit. As Ball pushed his throttle forward the Scout's engine roared in a deafening crescendo and the awe-struck Germans watched in dumb fury as the Scout darted across the field and lifted into the air. Rivetted to the spot they watched it circle the field while Ball leaned over the side of his cockpit and waved down at them. He had pulled off a brilliant piece of acting to turn the tables on them. Albert Ball would live to fight another day....and, after many more fights, to become one of Britain's greatest and most popular fighter aces.

The curious fact about this remarkable young pilot is that, although in the air he fought like a demon, on the ground he was a totally different character, reserved, solitary and deeply religious; a man with an inborn dislike of violence. Not for him the riotous mess parties that his fellow pilots regularly enjoyed. Never bragging of the number of 'kills' he had notched up, Ball was a 'loner' whose first love was playing his violin, and even the loudest artillery bombardment would not distract him from his music.

Ball's fellow pilots always knew where to find him if he was not flying. He would be strolling around the airfield, his violin tucked under his chin, playing some melancholy tune, or else he would be tending the little patch of garden he kept by the edge of the airfield. Yet when it came to a duel in the air there was no one who was a match for Ball, a thorough man who paid constant attention to detail and who, when not indulging in his two hobbies, would be supervising the servicing of his aircraft or stripping down his own machine-guns to ensure they were in perfect order.

The characteristics that went to make this supreme ace stemmed largely from his childhood days. Born in Nottingham in 1896, the son of the city's Mayor, he was a quiet, reserved boy whose shy ways and ready smile made him popular with everyone he met. He was not, however, a happy mixer and preferred to follow his boyhood passion for tinkering with old engines. He would strip them down completely and rebuild them from scratch. Indeed, he spent much of his time gathering bits and pieces of old engines and piecing them together to make new ones.

Once he found an old petrol engine to which he took a fancy but it was too heavy for him to move from the owner's yard. Undaunted, he raced home and borrowed his father's wheelbarrow to collect it. Wasting no time he got to work on it and within a week, what had been a corroded old wreck was thumping away in his back yard – working perfectly.

Another of Albert's passions was for guns and he built up quite a formidable collection. When he was not pottering about with old engines, he could be found on a nearby tennis court, firing off round after round of ammunition at a variety of targets. By the age of ten he was something of a crack-shot, with remarkable eyesight and very fast reactions.

Though he could not know it then, all these things were to
mean the difference between life and death to him in the
years to come.

At Trent College public school, where Albert was
educated, he was described by his headmaster as an 'undis-
tinguished pupil'. He was a dreamer and spent most of his
time advancing his knowledge of the combustion engine
rather than pursuing his academic studies. The result was
that, even when he left school, his spelling left a great deal to
be desired.

But while Albert Ball was tinkering with his engines, the
dark clouds of war were spreading over Europe. In the
Bosnian town of Sarajevo, the Archduke Ferdinand fell to an
assassin's bullet and Europe was plunged into war.

Albert was not yet twenty when the call to arms came.
Men from all walks of life flocked to the recruiting offices to
join the queues of volunteers. Among those who answered
the call was Albert Ball, who enlisted in the Sherwood
Foresters. He had not been with the Foresters long, however,
before he was posted to a cyclist unit near Ealing, on the
outskirts of London. It was there that he caught sight of his
first aircraft in flight, a flimsy biplane built of wood and
stretched canvas with a mass of struts and wire holding it
together.

Every day, these primitive machines flew over his unit
from the Royal Flying Corps aerodrome at Hendon. a few
miles away. Albert would gaze up, fascinated as they chugged
through the sky above him. To him these tiny aircraft were
more than just a marvel of man's inventive genius, they
represented a challenge and one that he found he could not
resist. He determined that he too would fly. But bitter
disappointment was not far off.

Albert had mistakenly thought that he had nothing more
to do than apply for a transfer to the Royal Flying Corps and
soon he would be wheeling through the air in one of their
brand new machines. The army authorities did not see things
that way. If he wanted to fly, he was told, he would have to
do it at his own expense. Among the army's leaders there was
much scepticism about the future and the effectiveness of the
R.F.C. for it had not yet proved its worth in battle.

Young Albert was downhearted but with that strain of
singlemindedness that was ingrained in him, he swore that he

would get his 'wings' – generals or no generals. Flying lessons, even in those days, were by no means cheap but after a long hard look at his bank balance and a decision to cut down drastically on his spending, he decided that he could just afford to take the course. Yet his troubles were only beginning. Another obstacle stood in his way – an irate sergeant-major who, like the generals, had little time for the R.F.C. and firmly believed that wars were to be won by soldiers and not by flying machines wheeling lazily about the skies.

'If you want to risk your flamin' neck in one o' them flyin' coffins, my lad, then good luck to you!' he thundered, 'but you'll do it in your own free time, not at the army's expense.'

Albert's only 'free time' was after lights-out at night or before parade at six o'clock in the morning. But he was not to be put off. As soon as he could, he duly enrolled as a student pilot at Hendon.

From then on, every morning before dawn, he pedalled off through the night on his bicycle to Hendon in time for a quick lesson then back again to Ealing in time for parade at six o'clock. The sergeant-major was far from pleased with the spectacle of the blear-eyed youth who presented himself on parade each morning but he could hardly help admiring the lad's spirit of determination.

Albert Ball's flying lessons were little short of nightmares for his instructor. Young Albert was no natural pilot and on several occasions he nearly came to grief. Wrecked under-carriages from bumpy and heavy landings were almost an everyday occurrence. The aeroplane on which he was learning was just not built to withstand Albert's kind of flying. His future as a pilot looked decidedly bleak – at least that was the way his instructor saw it. But not so Albert. What he lacked in flying skill he more than made up for in sheer enthusiasm and determination. At last, after a long series of near tragedies, Albert Ball got his wings on the 26th of January 1916. The Royal Flying Corps had gained a pilot of dubious skill and the army had lost a first-class cyclist!

Little more than a month later, without even time to 'polish' his flying, Ball was on board a troopship bound for France and the war. At last, he thought, he would have his chance. But when he arrived at the headquarters of Number

13 Squadron, he was in trouble almost at once. It was not that 13 was Albert's unlucky number but just that he was a thoroughly bad pilot. Major Marsh, the squadron commander, witnessed one of Albert's classic landings and was rendered almost speechless. Without delay, Lieutenant Ball was 'on the carpet'.

'Never,' Marsh proclaimed, 'have I seen such a shocking example of bad flying! It's a miracle you got down alive. I can't afford to have pilots like you in my squadron. I have no alternative but to recommend that you be sent back to England for further flying training.'

'But, sir,' Ball began....

'No "buts", Ball!' Marsh bellowed angrily. 'My mind is made up.'

Albert's heart sank at the prospect of being sent back to England without even having the opportunity of proving himself in battle. But fate was kind to the disillusioned young pilot. Before Marsh had a chance to put his threat into action, it was Albert's turn to take off on a reconnaissance mission over enemy territory, and that flight was to change his luck.

Flying a B.E.2c reconnaissance aircraft, he took off with five others. Ball and his observer, who manned the plane's only machine-gun, mounted in the front cockpit, were soon to get their first taste of aerial combat. The flimsy B.E.2cs which looked as if they might fall apart in a strong gust of wind, were slow and not at all easy to handle. They were certainly no match for the highly manoeuvrable German Fokker fighters and had come to grief so often that British pilots nick-named them 'Fokker Fodder'.

For the first time since his arrival in France he caught sight of the trenches which scarred the countryside far beneath him. That was a terrible battleground, where men died not only from bullets but from sheer exhaustion, drowning in the ever-present sea of mud.

The formation of British aircraft droned on over the scene of devastation below, crossing the German lines. At last Ball was in enemy territory and his heart beat faster as his eyes swept across the sky for signs of hostile aircraft. Every nerve in his body was taut with pent-up expectation. Suddenly one of the pilots in the formation waved frantically to the others and pointed into the sky above them. A pack of German fighters was hurtling down on them out of the clouds. Instantly the British pilots broke formation scattering in all directions, but one of the B.E.2cs was not quick enough and fell to a hail of bullets from a German's guns.

The fight that followed was short-lived — over almost before it had begun. As often happened in aerial battles, the sky was swarming with aircraft at one moment and empty the next. Ball found himself alone with no other aircraft in sight.

'Time we made ourselves scarce,' he yelled to his observer. 'Let's head for home.'

Ball wheeled the aircraft round in a tight turn and set course for his base. But as he did so, the engine gave a cough, a splutter, then stopped. Suddenly all was silent save for the whistle of the wind through the struts.

'What's up?' shouted the observer.

'Don't know,' Ball yelled back. 'We'll have to make a forced landing but I don't like the idea of putting her down on this side of the lines.'

Luckily Ball still had quite a bit of height so he scanned the countryside for a suitable landing place and glided gently down to make a bumpy touch-down in a field. The two men scrambled out of the aircraft. There was no sign of enemy troops and soon Ball's knowledge of engines was being put to the test.

Darkness came and, without light, Ball had to stop work on the repairs. He had no alternative but to wait until morning so he and the observer crouched in their respective cockpits and within minutes both were fast asleep.

With the coming of dawn, Ball got to work again on the engine and soon had it repaired. Airborne once more, they allowed themselves a sigh of relief.

But his troubles were far from over. Quite suddenly, the sky darkened and they flew into the teeth of a snowstorm. Again Ball was forced to land in an open field and wait until the snowstorm had passed. Then he took off once more and eventually succeeded in reaching his home base at eight o'clock in the morning.

As he scrambled down from his cockpit, he spotted a familiar figure striding purposefully towards him. It was Marsh, the commanding officer.

'Oh, oh! That's torn it,' he muttered to his observer. 'He's going to take me apart for turning up late. Looks like I'll be back in England sooner than I thought.'

But Albert's jaw dropped in some amazement when Marsh grabbed him by the hand and shook it heartily.

'Well done, Ball,' he said. 'We'd given you up for lost. I didn't think you had the stamina to bring her back. That's the sort of spirit we need – bags of guts and determination to succeed. Maybe you've got what it takes after all. I think you can forget about your trip to England now. With a bit of practice we'll make a pilot of you yet.'

Marsh turned on his heels and moved away.

'Well I'll be jiggered!' Albert exclaimed. 'And I was thinking I'd be on the next boat home. Marsh is not such a bad chap after all!'

Albert felt happier now that Marsh had more faith in him and with growing confidence, his flying improved quite dramatically. But he had yet to show his teeth in battle.

Ball's first victory in the air came on March 28th when he and Lieutenant Villiers, his observer, were on an artillery spotting mission near Givenchy, behind the German lines. As Villiers was scanning the countryside for signs of German gun emplacements, Ball spotted two enemy aircraft flying at 5000 feet a few miles away. He banked sharply and raced into the attack, warning Villiers to be ready for action as he did so.

As his B.E.2c closed in, Villiers opened up on one German aircraft with his machine-gun. His bullets thudded into the German's fuselage without seeming to have any effect. Then suddenly, a hail of bullets whistled past Ball's head and he realised they were being attacked by the other German aircraft. Determined not to let his 'prey' escape, Ball held the aircraft in position, allowing Villiers to continue pumping lead into the German. Suddenly Villiers' bullets found their mark and the German aircraft shot earthwards in a death dive. Only then did Ball take evasive action and roll away from the fusillade of bullets coming from the other German.

The remaining pilot, seeing his target slip away, broke off his attack and headed for home.

A jubilant pair of British fliers made for their base. But although elated by his success, Ball was slightly disappointed. He felt sure that, had he been on his own, without his observer to worry about, and in a more manoeuvrable fighter aircraft, he would have taken greater risks and could have shot down *both* aircraft. He felt that reconnaissance flying was tame stuff and longed to try his hand at flying a fighter.

He knew that there was a single-seater Bristol fighter attached to the squadron and itched to try it out. With that thought in mind he went to see Marsh.

At first, Marsh would not hear of it. He felt sure that Ball lacked the flying skill to handle a fighter. But Ball persisted and, eventually, Marsh relented. Permission was granted. With that, he lost no time in racing to the airstrip and clambering into the fighter's cockpit. As the aircraft bumped along the grass runway and lifted into the air, Ball knew at once that his proper place was in a fighter.

For the first time he felt completely in control of the aircraft. Soaring around the sky, looping, spinning and climbing, he put the fighter through its paces. At last he landed, exhilarated after the flight. He had found what he had been looking for.

But his luck was not to last. A fellow pilot took the squadron's one and only fighter up for a short training flight and crashed, wrecking the aircraft completely.

A week later another Bristol fighter was delivered to the squadron and Ball took off on a flight in it....a flight which was very nearly his last. Racing through the sky he decided to test the machine-gun mounted on the engine cowling in front of him. The gun was synchronised with the engine to fire through the rotating propeller, but something went wrong. Ball squeezed the trigger and instantly the propeller blades in front of him were shattered into a thousand pieces as the bullets ripped through them. The aircraft lurched out of control as it lost its forward speed and bits of propeller were thrown back at Ball. He ducked out of the way of the flying pieces of wood and fought furiously to regain control of the aircraft as it began to plunge earthwards. A scant few feet from the ground, he succeeded in pulling it out of the dive and levelled off to land. He heaved a sigh of relief as the aircraft slid to a halt. He had experienced a close shave and it was not to be the last one in a fighting career destined to amaze the world.

Ball's career as a reconnaissance pilot was far from impressive. After his flights in the Bristol fighter he thought of nothing else but being posted to a fighter squadron. Day

after day he pestered Marsh for a transfer until on May 7th, it
came. He was to report to Number 11 Squadron where he
would fly Nieuport Scouts.

Ball was filled with excitement when he arrived at his new
squadron and was 'introduced' to the Nieuport he was to fly.
He looked it over carefully and the more he saw of it, the
more he liked it.

The Nieuport Scout was a small, single-seater biplane of
French design powered by a big, 110 horsepower Le Rhône
nine-cylinder air-cooled engine which drove a two bladed
propeller. It was built entirely of wood covered with
stretched canvas and it had one distinct advantage over other
biplanes. The lower set of wings was narrower than the upper
set, giving the pilot a considerably better view downwards
and allowing him better vision in battle. Mounted on the
centrepiece of the upper wings was a Lewis machine-gun.

Ball ran his fingers along the trim lines of the fuselage and
knew instinctively that this was the aircraft for him. He was
unaware of it then, but a partnership was being formed which
would strike terror into the hearts of the German pilots and
wipe the 'Fokker Scourge' from the air.

Within days he was in action. He threw himself into battle
with absolute abandon, flying headlong into enemy formations with guns chattering, terrifying the enemy with his
boldness.

Ball was determined that his opponents should know
whom they were fighting when he engaged them in battle, so
he attached a bright red spinner to the hub of his propeller
and it was not long before the Germans were fleeing at the
very sight of the red-nosed fighter screaming towards them.
The risks he took were such that in the first few weeks of his
career as a fighter pilot he was shot down no less than *six*
times but on every occasion he managed to land his machine
on the right side of the lines.

Ball's daring in battle stemmed from one thing alone. He
had an unshakable faith in God. Every night before retiring
to bed he said his prayers and firmly believed that in battle
he was protected by the hand of the Almighty. His faith
drove him on to uncanny feats of daring and he grabbed
every opportunity of getting into the air and into a fight. He
would think nothing of returning from a mission, usually
having shot down an enemy plane and with his aircraft

punctured with bullet holes, quickly refuelling and then immediately taking off again. His energy seemed limitless.

On one occasion he returned to his base covered from head to toe in oil, and with his Scout's fuselage ripped apart with bullet holes and its elevator controls almost shot to pieces. Without hesitation he borrowed a piece of rag from his mechanic, wiped his coat and goggles clean of oil, made some quick repairs to the aircraft then was airborne again, leaving behind a group of staggered onlookers.

Ball's score of 'kills' in the air was mounting rapidly. The newspapers at home carried banner headlines and gripping stories of his daring in the air. In recognition of his bravery he was admitted to the Distinguished Service Order and awarded the Military Cross for Gallantry. But he was driving himself to the limit and his commander saw this. Ball was ordered home – and there he had to face another ordeal – for by now he was a national hero and was expected to live up to it. In his native Nottingham, for instance, the reluctant hero was made a Freeman of the city and such public appearances scared him far more than the sight of a flight of Fokkers.

To make matters worse, the Royal Flying Corps found another use for him, instructing newly-qualified pilots in the art of aerial combat tactics. Soon he was thoroughly bored with this new job, longing to get back to France and into action again. He pestered his commander to allow him to return but it was only after weeks of pleading that his request was finally granted. He took off for France once more. It was to be for the last time.

Crossing the French coast, Ball wasted no time in getting back into the fight. Before reporting his return, he decided to take a quick trip over the enemy lines....just to let the Germans know he was back. As he did so, he spotted a formation of enemy aircraft and launched his usual bold attack. Roaring in, he shot down two of them before hurrying on to base to report his arrival. Albert Ball, by then a captain, was once more in the fight.

Within hours of his return he was in the air again, high over the lines, with his guns taking their deadly toll. His hair-raising methods were paying off but he was not to have it all his own way....

Once, while flying alone over his favourite hunting ground

behind the German lines, he caught sight of twelve enemy planes and charged headlong into the formation, shooting down three of them. Out of ammunition, he sped back to a nearby British airfield, grabbed a fresh supply of drums of ammunition and took off again.

This time, however, he was attacked by a group of fourteen fighters. They swarmed around him like bees, pumping bullets into his Nieuport. The barrage of fire ripped through the aircraft, shattering control lines, smashing his rear-view mirror and windscreen, blasting away struts and worst of all severing a fuel line. Instantly petrol poured out of the broken line.

'One spark,' he thought, 'and that will be it. I've got to get out of here...and the faster the better!'

Miraculously, he managed to escape and landed on the right side of the lines. He repaired his wrecked aircraft and for the second time in only a few months, curled up in his cockpit and dozed off to sleep. The following morning he took off and returned to base. His comrades stared at him in disbelief. They had thought him dead. Surely he must 'cop it' one day they thought. But Ball continued to reign supreme. Then, one day, he met his match....

While flying on a patrol he sighted a German single-seater fighter. Both pilots turned on each other and the fight began but try as they might, neither of them could gain the advantage of the other. Each of them used every trick in the book but neither Ball nor the German could get into a position to deliver the final, fatal blow. At last having used all their ammunition, they both realised that the fight could end in nothing better than a draw. Simultaneously, they both burst into peels of laughter and waved in admiration to each other before parting and heading home. Ball never did discover who his friendly rival was.

Apart from that one brave pilot, no one would intentionally do battle with Ball. The sight of the red spinner was enough to send most Germans scurrying for home. This, however did not please Ball who itched for a good scrap. Audaciously, he would zoom low over enemy airfields taunting the German pilots, inviting them to come up for a fight. But they knew his reputation and almost always refused. It seemed that no one would ever get the better of this magnificent fighter pilot. But on the evening of the 7th of May 1917, someone did.

To this day, no one knows for certain how Albert Ball met his death. On that fateful May evening he took off on patrol in an S.E.5 fighter. After a furious dog-fight in which many aircraft were lost, his aeroplane was seen to disappear into cloud. Later the S.E.5 was found wrecked near Annoeullin, not far from Lens behind the German lines. Ball lay dead in the cockpit.

There are many theories about how he died. Some say he was shot down by Lothar von Richthofen, the younger brother of Germany's greatest ace, Baron Manfred von Richthofen. Others say that he was shot in the head by a German sharp-shooter hidden in the tower of a church in Annoeullin as he swept past in a low dive. There are also accounts of the incident that say he was completely overwhelmed by more than twenty German fighters and could not escape their guns. Whatever the truth is, one thing is certain, he died the way he fought – bravely and alone.

The Germans buried him with full military honours in the Cemetery of Honour at Annoeullin and carved a laurel leaf on his cross which bore these words:

'He gave his life for his fatherland.'

In his short but spectacular career, Ball had shot down forty-four enemy aircraft in more than one hundred and fifty air battles and helped change the tide of war in the air. His courage and daring lived on as a fine example to the many Allied pilots who were to follow him.

On July 22nd, 1917, Captain Albert Ball, D.S.O. and two Bars, M.C. was posthumously awarded his country's highest decoration for bravery – the Victoria Cross.

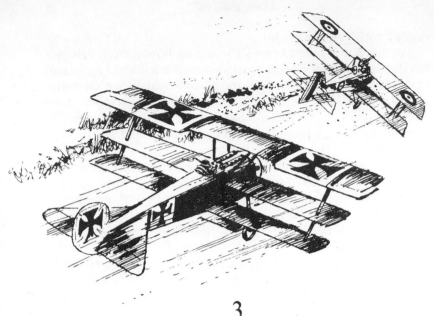

3
The Red Baron

Of all the fighter pilots who fought their duels in the war-torn skies over Europe during the First World War, one man reigned supreme. He was Rittmeister Baron Manfred von Richthofen, leader of the renowned 'Richthofen Circus'. Flying a bright red Fokker Triplane or Albatros, he destroyed more enemy aircraft than any other pilot in the war and in doing so carved a name for himself among the immortals of the air.

Richthofen was a born hunter. As a child on his father's estate in Silesia, he spent endless hours stalking wild animals amongst the trees of the forest. He soon became a shot of almost uncanny accuracy; a skill that was to give him the edge over his opponents in the air, years later. He lived for the hunt and the excitement of ultimate victory over an untamed beast gave young Richthofen his greatest satisfaction. But these early days of freedom amid the forests were not to last.

It was the custom in aristocratic Prussian families for the eldest son to become a military cadet and eventually join the ranks of the *élite* officer corps. So it was that at the age of eleven, Manfred took his place at a famous military school.

Discipline at the school was incredibly strict and the young cadet hated it. He continually pined for the day when he would return to his father's estate and roam the forest, pitting his wits against the wild boar and deer. Often he would lie awake at night and relive a successful hunt, but for too long the hunt had to remain a dream.

At last the time came when he was transferred to the War Academy in Berlin where life changed for him. At the Academy he was taught more soldierly pursuits, like battle tactics, military strategy and history, but above all he learned the importance of being a Prussian officer, a man singled out to command.

He emerged from the Academy a proud, erect young lieutenant; every inch the professional soldier. He was given to arrogance but displayed the correctness of manner expected of a Prussian officer.

Richthofen joined the 1st Regiment of Uhlans, the cream of the German cavalry. Excelling as a horseman he soon made a name for himself riding in steeplechases where he won many trophies. The dashing, handsome young Prussian was the envy of his fellow officers and revelled in the new-found fame which fed a hungry ego. But the gay life of the young officer was not to last long, for soon the entire continent was plunged into war.

As battles began to take place and the mock conflicts became a reality, the toll of dead mounted at an alarming rate. Horsemen were cut down in their thousands by the new rapid-fire machine-guns used by the Allies, and Richthofen was quick to realise that the cavalry charge had become a thing of the past. Not averse to voicing this belief amongst his fellow officers, he did his popularity little good in a crack cavalry regiment.

In time Richthofen was duly transferred to an infantry regiment where he was given a desk job, organising the supply of war materials to the front. To the ambitious glory-seeking Richthofen this was the ultimate insult. He failed to grasp the importance of his job and soon became embittered and frustrated, longing for action. Then one day while he walked glumly near his barracks, pondering on his lot, an incident occurred which was to change his life and ultimately bring him the glory and fame he sought so desperately.

As he pondered on his unpromising future, the sound of racing aircraft engines reached his ears. He glanced upwards and caught sight of a flight of German reconnaissance aircraft gracefully sweeping through the sky, en route for a mission over enemy lines. His eyes followed them until they were lost to view. Then he turned back towards his quarters with fresh life in his step. His mind was buzzing with excitement. He had found what he had been looking for — a new mount with which to go into battle — the aeroplane.

The potential of the aeroplane as a weapon of war was not lost upon Richthofen and with the prospect of fresh glory to be won he applied for a transfer to the German Army Air Service. His request was granted.

In those early days of the two-seater reconnaissance aircraft the observer was in command and the pilot was regarded as little more than a glorified chauffeur. It was natural, therefore, that young Richthofen should choose to become an observer. After a short training, he qualified as an observer, manning the gun in the rear of a two-seater.

He and his pilot were soon flying on operational missions over the enemy lines and, on one of these sorties, Richthofen succeeded in shooting down his first victim, but he was far from satisfied. He had not been able to confirm the 'kill' because the aircraft had crashed behind the British lines, and therefore he could not claim it as a victory. But rather than blame himself for this he accused his pilot of not holding the aircraft in position long enough for him, Richthofen, to finish off the enemy plane while it was still over German territory.

It was then that he made up his mind that the only way in which he could score more kills would be to pilot the aircraft *himself* and be in command. Back he went to flying school, this time to train as a pilot. But he was far from prepared for what was in store for him. Flying the almost primitive aircraft in service at that time required considerable skill and the young Prussian found it extremely difficult to acquire that skill. For him, even the very basic requirements of flying like taking off and landing were nightmares, and his instructor almost gave up hope of ever being able to teach him to fly.

Richthofen's career as a pilot very nearly ended before it

had begun and the future looked distinctly bleak for the would-be ace. Furthermore he tended to pay little attention to the lessons he was taught on the theory of flight, the basic principles of how and why aeroplanes fly. The upshot was that he failed his qualifying examinations more than once. In spite of this he was determined to succeed and finally, after more than twenty flights as a pupil pilot he managed to go solo....only to come to grief on landing. The plane was a complete write-off – but luckily Richthofen survived.

Undeterred by what had happened he tried again and again until finally perseverance won the day and he gained his pilot's badge.

In March 1916, he was posted to the front, only to find that he was still to be flying in the cumbersome reconnaissance machines and not the sleek fighters he had hoped for. Richthofen was downhearted but he had a flash of brilliance. He attached an additional machine-gun to the upper wing of his aircraft just above the cockpit so that both he and his observer could fire at the enemy. Then, in his airborne battleship, he took off on patrol, hunting once more, eager to seek out his prey.

On his first few missions he was to meet with disappointment, but then on a bright, clear day he took to the air and over the enemy lines caught sight of a French Scout plane not far off....

His eyes lit up as he wheeled the aircraft round for the attack and his heart raced as he swept down on the unsuspecting scout. He had not been spotted by the Frenchman and as he closed in he prepared to fire. But to do this he had to *stand up* in the cockpit and hold the control column between his knees to guide the aircraft while he clutched the machine-gun! For someone whose flying ability using two hands left a great deal to be desired, this was no easy matter.

Richthofen closed an eye and peered through the gun sight then his finger curled round the trigger and squeezed when the enemy aircraft filled the sight. Instantly Richthofen's aircraft shook as the machine-gun burst into life, pumping bullets into the Frenchman. He fell back into his seat as the scout erupted into a great ball of fire and jagged pieces of aircraft hurtled past him.

Richthofen felt a wave of triumph sweep through him as

the shattered remnants of the enemy aircraft cascaded towards the ground. At last he had done it. His brainwave had, he felt, proved successful and he chalked up his confirmed victory. But his invention was not to prove quite as successful as he had hoped. Because he had to stand in the cockpit while firing his machine-gun, it became almost impossible to manoeuvre the aircraft. It was also particularly dangerous as he had to undo his seatbelt before standing, which made it all too easy to fall out of the unstable aeroplane. But a new and deadly innovation was on its way.

A young Dutch aircraft designer, Anthony Fokker, perfected a device which was to revolutionise fighting aircraft and turn the tide of the war in the air in favour of the German Air Service. He mounted a machine-gun on top of the nose of an aircraft, just behind the propeller and synchronised the firing mechanism of the gun with the engine so that the bullets passed between the propeller blades. This meant that the pilot could remain seated while attacking an enemy and merely point the aircraft in the direction of his opponent's plane and fire.

Within weeks of the new machine-gun being fitted to German aircraft, British and French planes were being knocked out of the skies like so many swatted flies. The slow and cumbersome Allied aeroplanes proved no match for the fast manoeuvrable German machines with their forward-firing machine-guns. (It was not until much later when the Allied pilots were supplied with synchronised machine-guns and more lively aircraft that they could do battle with the Germans on level terms.)

Meanwhile the German Air Service was equipped with the latest fighter, the single-seater Albatros, armed with twin Spandau forward-firing machine-guns. The combination of this superbly designed new fighter and the synchronised guns was even more deadly than the greatest optimist could have hoped for and for some time the Royal Flying Corps took a terrible beating in the air. With its 160 hp Mercedes engine, the Albatros was far superior to any Allied fighter. It was not only highly manoeuvrable but had a top speed of 103 miles an hour, a ceiling of 18,000 feet and a flying endurance of two hours. This was the machine Richthofen had been waiting for and he longed to get into battle with one of these new aircraft.

In the summer of 1916, Richthofen met Oswald Boelke, then the supreme champion of the German aces. Boelke was a skilled tactician with a formidable list of victories to his credit. When he met young Richthofen he was not at all impressed by his skill as a pilot but he was staggered at his remarkable accuracy with a gun. Boelke reckoned he could cure the glaring faults in Richthofen's flying and asked him to join his squadron. Richthofen accepted the offer instantly. He wanted more than anything else to study the veteran ace at close quarters and learn all he could.

Richthofen duly joined Boelke's squadron and flew with him on many missions, watching his every move, imitating him but also improving where he could upon the ace's technique. Boelke's basic approach to aerial combat was simple but effective. He would hold his formation in a tight pack and charge into the enemy like a ramrod, smashing its formation, confusing and un-nerving the enemy pilots. The German pilots could then pick off the bewildered enemy at will.

Richthofen's score of kills in the air soon began to mount rapidly as his cunning improved. He applied the same skill to stalking his prey in the air as he had used so many years before in the forests of his father's estate in Silesia — and it worked.

It was customary in those days for a pilot's comrades to present him with a trophy when he shot down an enemy but this was not quite good enough for Richthofen. He had to outdo his fellows and go a step farther. Whenever *he* won a battle in the air he presented *himself* with an inscribed silver cup to commemorate the victory. If he happened to shoot down two enemies in one day he would have two cups made and so it went on. It was not long before his room displayed a formidable array of cups and souvenirs of his kills. But the vain Richthofen's insatiable desire for fame was a long way from being fully satisfied. While the other great German aces received wide publicity in the German newspapers and were national heroes, Richthofen's achievements remained unsung. He had yet to achieve the triumph he had dreamed of so many times....shooting down an enemy ace. Then on November 23rd 1916, his dream became reality when he came face to face in the air with one of Britain's greatest aces, Major Laneo Hawker V.C., a brilliant aerial duellist.

On that fateful day, Richthofen and his squadron were airborne and heading for the Bapaume area of France near Amiens where heavy fighting was taking place between German and Allied ground forces. The squadron had been alerted that there were British reconnaissance planes in the area observing German troop movements and these had to be stopped at all cost, for they were relaying this vital information back to the heavy artillery which in turn was plastering the area with shell fire. The two-seater British observation planes were 'easy meat' for the German Albatroses which could out-manoeuvre and out-gun them. Richthofen knew this, but so did the British and while Richthofen and his squadron were racing towards Bapaume with the prospect of some easy game, Major Hawker was leading a squadron of D.H.2 fighters into the air to act as cover for the reconnaissance aircraft. The clash was inevitable.

The D.H.2 aircraft which Hawker flew must have been one of the strangest machines ever to take to the air. It was a 'pusher' which meant that the propeller was positioned behind the wings and instead of pulling the aircraft through the air it pushed it along. The position of the propeller behind the single seat cockpit had, however, one great advantage. It allowed the pilot to use a forward-firing machine-gun. The cockpit and the engine housing appeared to be the only solid pieces of the aircraft, apart from the wings, for the rear half of the fuselage consisted only of metal tubing strengthened by struts in a tapering box-like shape with a small tail stuck on the end in what seemed like an afterthought. Nevertheless, in spite of its frail appearance, the D.H.2 was a sturdy and manoeuvrable aeroplane, liked by the pilots who flew it. Still, it was certainly no match for the Albatros and the odds were very much in favour of the Germans.

When the clash came, Hawker was singled out for attention by Richthofen himself, although at that time, the German had no idea that he was about to join in battle with a top British ace. The clash that ensued was one of the classic aerial battles of all time.

The two pilots threw their aircraft around the sky. each one desperately trying to outwit the other and deliver that fatal burst of fire that would seal the fate of his opponent.

They twisted, turned, dived and zoomed using every trick in the book to gain the advantage. The exhausting pace of the battle was telling on both men and each of them knew only too well that the slightest lapse in concentration would mean certain death for him.

Hawker was without doubt the superior pilot but Richthofen had a vastly superior machine with greater speed which could get him out of trouble quickly and with ease. The fierce conflict continued until Hawker threw his machine into a dive for the ground. Down it hurtled with Richthofen on its tail then, a scant few feet from the ground, Hawker levelled off and shot across the fields with Richthofen still in hot pursuit.

Richthofen peered through his gunsight until, for an instant, Hawker's machine was there, framed in the sight. That was enough for the German. He jabbed the trigger of his Spandau and a hail of bullets thudded into Hawker's machine. The Englishman didn't have a chance. He could not escape the fusillade of fire so close to the ground. Suddenly, his aircraft lurched, keeled over and plunged to earth. He was killed instantly.

Richthofen circled the wreckage, overcome with jubilation, then roared off for home to a tumultuous welcome from his comrades. At last he had fulfilled the ambition he had cherished so long and news of his victory soon spread like wildfire, with every newspaper in Germany proclaiming his mastery of the air.

It was not long before Richthofen became a legend on both sides of the lines. After only one year in action, he was given command of his own squadron. Now he set out to gather around him the finest pilots in the German Air Service and the legendary 'Richthofen Circus' was born.

To make absolutely sure that his squadron was instantly recognisable as the Circus, he painted his own aircraft bright red and insisted that all the other aircraft in the squadron be predominantly red. It was because of this that he gained the nickname, 'The Red Baron'.

All the pilots of the Circus were hand-picked by Richthofen himself and he took great pains to coach them in aerial battle tactics.

'Always attack from a position of strength,' he would tell his pilots. He hardly ever attacked an enemy formation larger than his own and he always attacked out of the sun, so that the enemy pilots would be blinded by the sun's rays when they looked up to see their attackers.

Richthofen spent hours studying captured Allied aircraft, working out their weak points and the most effective way of attacking them. For instance, the old British scout planes had a 'blind spot' beneath the tail where neither the pilot nor the observer could see an attacking aircraft. Richthofen soon made use of this discovery with devastating effect.

As the number of his trophies mounted, so the Richthofen legend grew. But in spite of his fantastic successes in the air, Richthofen was no dare-devil. He always chose the weakest aircraft in an enemy formation, leaving the rest to the other pilots in his squadron. A damaged plane or a 'lame duck', one with engine trouble, was fair game for the Baron and he had an uncanny knack of sensing that a pilot was 'raw' and new to the game.

As his fame spread, Richthofen was showered with decorations, but his crowning glory came when he was awarded his country's highest decoration for bravery, the *Pour le Mérite*, the German equivalent of the Victoria Cross. By then he had more than sixty aircraft to his credit and he was given command of a fighter wing.

Daily he faced death in the air but by some miracle he always returned to base unscathed. His comrades believed that he was unbeatable in the air and indeed Richthofen began to believe that himself. But his feeling of infallibility was soon to be badly jolted.

On the 6th of July, he and his Circus took off on a hunting patrol. After a short while in the air, they spotted a squadron of British aircraft and they engaged the enemy. The dog-fight that followed lasted for more than half an hour and Richthofen felt ill-at-ease because he had become too deeply involved in the fight. He much preferred to make a quick kill then head for home but this time he was not getting the chance. He was penned in amongst a gaggle of battling aircraft. The sky was full of planes twisting and turning, with burning aircraft hurtling towards the ground leaving trails of black smoke which scarred the blue sky.

Then as Richthofen was about to attack a British aircraft, Albert Woodbridge, a young R.F.C. observer, fired a burst at the Red Baron's aircraft from long range. In the dying seconds of its flight, one of the bullets hit Richthofen's leather flying helmet, ripping it open and gashing his head. He passed out instantly and his machine hurtled out of control towards the ground. Miraculously he regained consciousness a few hundred feet from the ground but to his horror could not see. Blood from his wound was streaming over and into his goggles and he tore at them desperately and succeeded in ripping them off. Gaping in terror at the ground as it loomed up in front of him he instinctively hauled back on the control column and the plane responded, levelling off only seconds before slithering along the ground and coming to a halt.

Fortunately Richthofen had landed in German territory and was dragged from the wreckage by German troops and rushed to hospital. Luckily too he was not seriously wounded, but this incident had a dramatic effect upon him. He had escaped death by a hair's breadth and from that moment onwards he, like so many other fighter pilots, began to suffer from terrible nightmares in which he relived the horror of his narrow escape.

Richthofen went on three months' convalescent leave but when he finally returned to the front, he was a changed man. Gone was his air of over-confidence and in its place was a fear that death must inevitably catch up with him. Worse still, the tide of battle on the front had swung in favour of the Allies.

The Royal Flying Corps had been equipped with the new single-seater Sopwith Camel aircraft which was to prove the greatest fighter of the First World War. Powered by a 130 hp Clerget engine, it had a maximum speed of 115 m.p.h and a ceiling of 19,000 feet. Most important of all, though, it could out-manoeuvre anything else in the sky and had two forward-firing Vickers machine-guns mounted just in front of the cockpit. The R.F.C. could now fight on more than equal terms with the German Air Service.

Richthofen's squadrons, on the other hand, were taking delivery of the new Fokker Triplanes, one of which was to become the Baron's favourite mount in battle. The performance of this three winged aircraft was not greatly different from that of the Sopwith Camel but the Camel did have a slight edge over it.

As the days went by more and more German aircraft were falling to British guns and many of the German aces were killed in action or cracked up under the strain of battle. Now Richthofen had to make do with young and inexperienced pilots in his Circus and he spent more and more uneasy nights. He was by this time twenty-six years old. As the days passed his fear of death grew, but to his credit he continued to force himself into battle so as not to lose face in front of his comrades. On the 20th of April 1918, he notched up his eightieth victory — his last!

On the morning of the 21st April 1918 the Richthofen Circus took off from its base at Cappy, led by the Red Baron in his Fokker Triplane. As they approached the British lines they were joined by yet another eighteen German planes combining to make a formidable task force.

About that same time, a group of Royal Air Force Camels of 209 Squadron rose into the air from their base on a routine patrol. Crouched in the cockpit of one of the Camels was a twenty-four year old Canadian pilot, Captain Roy Brown. He was already an ace with twelve victories to his credit but on this flight he was to become the leading figure in one of the greatest air mysteries of the century.

As the German force roared on, Richthofen spotted a flight of British reconnaissance aircraft far below his formation and ordered four of his pilots to attack. They dived on the British aircraft and a furious battle began. But just as their guns roared into life, Roy Brown's squadron came on the scene and went to the aid of the Scouts. Seeing this, Richthofen ordered his entire force into action. The result was a battle on an immense scale.

Soon the sky was filled with aircraft, careering through the air, twisting and turning on each other with guns chattering. In the maze of mud-filled trenches below, gunners and infantrymen of the Australian army watched the bee-like aircraft buzzing about the sky.

Richthofen wove in and out of the *melée* of aircraft looking for an easy kill. Suddenly he saw one and zoomed in on its tail. The British pilot, Second Lieutenant May, glanced round and saw the red Fokker bearing down on him. He dived, climbed, rolled, banked and did all he could to shake off the German but the Red Baron would not let go.

May, convinced that his end was near, shot towards the ground in a last, desperate bid to escape his attacker's guns and levelled off between the high banks of a river. The Red

Baron screeched after him with his throttle wide open, squeezing every ounce of power out of the Fokker.

High above, Roy Brown watched the 'cat and mouse' chase and dived in behind Richthofen's machine. The German, forgetting the first rule of aerial fighting by not keeping a watch on his tail, failed to see Brown's machine charging in on him. His eyes were fixed on the helpless Camel ahead of him. He was just about to squeeze the trigger when Brown levelled off behind him and fired a burst at the triplane. Instantly Richthofen jerked upright in his cockpit. A bullet had smashed through his chest, killing him immediately. Brown banked away sharply, leaving the Fokker to slither along the ground and come to a halt in front of the Australian trenches.

The Aussies raced towards the aircraft where they found the pilot sitting upright and motionless in the cockpit with a hand still clutching the control column. He was lifted gently from the cockpit and laid on the ground, then an officer went through the dead airman's pockets. The lieutenant's jaw fell in stunned amazement when he read the name on the identity card.

'It's Richthofen!' he gasped.

With that the soldiers pounced on the aircraft, tearing it to pieces to get souvenirs. Before the lieutenant could stop his men they had stripped the aircraft almost bare of its canvas, controls and instrument panel.

Roy Brown was officially credited with shooting down the Red Baron but later, when a post mortem was carried out on the body, a strange fact came to light. The bullet which had killed him – the only one to hit his body – had entered into the *side* of his chest. This posed one very important question. How could Brown, who had been firing at Richthofen from *behind* have shot him on the *side* of the chest? It is possible that the fatal bullet may have ricocheted off some metal object in the cockpit but by then it was impossible to say, since the aircraft had been stripped clean by the souvenir hunters.

Was it Brown who shot the Red Baron, or was it someone else who fired the fatal shot? The answer will probably never be known for certain. Many claims to the distinction have been made but the most convincing alternative came from an Australian infrantryman who was positioned on the river bank

level with Richthofen's aircraft when it flew past. He loosed
off a wild shot. Was that the bullet which killed Richthofen?

Like the deaths of Captain Albert Ball V.C. and of many
others who fought in the troubled skies over Europe, the
mystery is likely to remain unsolved for ever. Over the years
since that fateful day in 1918, followers of the Baron's
career have reconstructed the action which took place but
none has been able to come up with any conclusive proof one
way or the other. The R.A.F., however, has never been in any
doubt as to who put paid to the Red Baron, Roy Brown's old
squadron, No. 209, still carries on its crest a red eagle
(symbolising Richthofen's aircraft) falling out of the sky.

Richthofen was buried by the Australians with full
military honours and a few days later an R.A.F. aircraft
swooped low over his base and dropped a canister which
contained the following message....

'To the German Flying Corps. Rittmeister Baron Manfred
von Richthofen was killed in aerial combat on April 21st,
1918. He was buried with full military honours. From the
British Royal Air Force.'

Seven months later, the war ended. Today it is the name of
von Richthofen which is remembered more than any other
from that terrible conflict. That is how the Red Baron would
have wanted it.

4

The Ace with One Eye

Edward 'Mick' Mannock was pre-eminently a fighter. Dubbed the 'Mad Major' by those who saw him in action, he had a burning hatred for his enemy, the German Army Air Service. Unlike Albert Ball who had a distinct distaste for killing his enemy, Mannock's one aim was to knock as many German aeroplanes out of the sky as he could and, hopefully, to kill their crews at the same time. As he saw it, his job as a fighter pilot during the First World War was to annihilate the enemy....and this he did with such success that he became the top-scoring British ace in the process and was hailed by many as being the greatest fighter tactician the British air force has ever had. He was certainly the most successful.

Mannock's ruthlessness undoubtedly stemmed from a pitifully cruel childhood and the terrible privations he suffered then. But there was one other factor which played a major part in forming his character....he was blind in one eye. Not, one would think, the ideal combination of characteristics which go to make a top-scoring fighter pilot — but they did.

Edward, nicknamed 'Mick', Mannock, was born in the Cavalry Barracks of the Royal Scots Greys at Brighton, in 1889, the son of an n.c.o. in the Second Inniskilling Dragoons. Both his parents were Irish, a fact which endowed Mick with the fighting spirit which was to play such a big part in his later life. While still a young boy, Mick was taken to India, where his father had been posted for garrison duty. It was about this time that he contracted a strange illness which left him almost blind in his left eye.

Mannock's father was a rough diamond, a spendthrift and a particularly brutal type of person who cared absolutely nothing for his family. He had a fiery temper and often flew into a rage at the slightest provocation, taking out his frustrations on the family. Violent rows were an everyday occurrence in the Mannock household and Mick had to bear much of the brunt of his father's dislike for family life. His mother did what she could to protect Mick and the rest of the children from the wrath of their father but without a great deal of success. The atmosphere that prevailed in the household was sombre and left a lasting impression upon Mick.

To escape from the bitter reality of his home life, Mick turned inwards, becoming a silent, reserved child given to spending long hours reading or wandering in the country studying animal and bird life. He found it difficult to communicate with other children and saw himself as an outsider, shunned by all those around him, partly because of his defective eyesight but also because of his rather frail and weak appearance.

At last, Mick's father was sent off to the Boer War which was raging in South Africa and at least then, one of the boy's problems was removed though it was replaced by another, intense poverty. His mother took him and the other children back to England on a troopship. By then the eyesight in his left eye had almost completely gone and he could only see properly with his right eye.

During the long voyage home to England, Mick's mother noticed that he shunned the opportunities to play with the other boys on the ship and was continually at odds with them. She was heartbroken but there was little she could do. Back in England, the family settled down in Canterbury but the comparative peace of home life without his tempestuous father did little to draw Mick out of himself.

Then his father returned from the war and the continual family rows broke out again, until at last the father resolved to leave the British Army and seek his fortune elsewhere. Without hesitation or a thought for the well-being of his family he deserted them and left them to fend for themselves. They were poverty stricken, without savings and with little likelihood of money coming into the household to provide for their vital needs. Mick, his brother Patrick and his two sisters were clad in cast-off clothing and often walked shoeless about the streets. In order to try and make ends meet and provide some kind of income, Patrick succeeded in getting a clerical job.

The bare necessities of life were essential. Mrs. Mannock could not afford to allow Mick to remain at school and at the age of thirteen he left to find a job and help as best he could to add to the family income. But work was hard to come by and he spent many weary hours plodding the streets in search of it. At last he found a job of sorts, working in a greengrocer's shop lugging hundred-weight bags of potatoes from early morning till late at night for the meagre pittance of two shillings and sixpence a week. It was not unusual for Mick to return home at night utterly exhausted, with cut and blistered hands.

Soon he left the greengrocer and got a job in a local barber's shop, lathering the customers' faces and sweeping up around the shop. Now his wages were doubled. He earned the princely sum of five shillings a week and with things not quite as hard as they had been was able to turn his attention to enjoying himself with the occasional game of cricket. His bowling, however, was far from accurate and Mick knew that the reason for this was his blindness, though he would never admit it to his team-mates.

For some time now his brother Patrick had been trying to persuade Mick to find a clerical job but he hated the prospect of sitting at a desk for the rest of his life. However, times were hard and he was eventually persuaded to give it a try and joined the National Telephone Company at Canterbury. For Mick the job was boring beyond belief and he itched to get into something more active, so in due course he applied to be taken on as a telephone linesman. To his delight his request was granted and he was sent to Wellingborough, in Northamptonshire, to learn the tricks of the trade.

It was there that two significant things happened to him. Firstly he joined the local branch of the Territorial Army where he was taught first aid by the R.A.M.C. The second was that he met Jim Eyles, an older likable man who struck up an instant friendship with the boy. They always got on well together and eventually Mick moved into lodgings with Eyles and his wife. He quickly took to life in their family and had soon 'adopted' Jim Eyles as his second father. At long last he was given the affection he had not had from his own father and the change in young Mick was soon noticeable.

But the wanderlust was in Mick and he determined to see the world. Eyles lent him some money, and with it he travelled to Turkey where he was given a contract to supervise the installation of telephone lines in some of the more remote regions of the country. In Turkey he made quite a number of friends amongst the British community but he soon became homesick and the climate in that country was not entirely to his liking. He longed to be back in the comfort of the Eyles' home in Wellingborough and his chance to get there was to come sooner than he imagined. It was 1914 and when war came to Europe the Turks sided with the Germans. Mick found himself in a hostile country where he and all other British people were thrown into internment prisons.

Determined to get out of prison, Mick played on the fact that he was blind in one eye. The Turks accepted his story and classed him as a non-combatant, incapable of taking part in active service. Had they had the power of second sight they would have kept him securely under lock and key for the duration of the war. Instead he was duly released and returned to England.

There he re-enlisted in the Territorials with the Royal Army Medical Corps. But Mick did not view the passive role of a medical orderly with any relish. He wanted to be in the thick of the fight and he applied for a transfer to the Royal Engineers which was granted. He was commissioned but quickly became disenchanted with this too. It was only as a result of a chance meeting with an old friend that he finally decided upon what he wanted to do. His friend had recently joined the Royal Flying Corps and was undergoing pilot training at the time. When he related some of his stories of flying, they immediately caught Mannock's imagination. Men like Ball were making their names in the skies over Europe really hitting hard at the enemy and this was all Mannock wanted to do. He resolved then to apply for a transfer but there was one big problem. How could he ever pass the stiff medical examination with only one good eye. His friend had a look at the eye and pointed out that it appeared just the same as the other. In fact he had been fooled. If Mick could fool his friends, then why couldn't he fool the medical officer who was to examine him?

Mannock's application for a transfer was granted and he joined the R.F.C., but the day soon came when he had to go for the medical examination. Before the appointed hour, however, he sneaked into the medical room while no one was there and memorised the letters on the eye chart which was to be used for the eye test. When he was eventually asked to read from the board he rattled off the letters faultlessly and was passed as fit! He had, he thought, got over his biggest hurdle. But higher hurdles were still before him. He had not yet been in the air and tried the business of flying.

Mick Mannock's flying training began and it was soon pretty obvious that he was no 'natural' pilot. Because of his defective eyesight, he made some incredible mistakes in the air with hair-raising results. The upshot was that he spent much time in front of his commanding officer being lectured about his clumsy and inept flying. Then one day during his training one of the greatest aces of the First World War arrived at the base to give the students instruction in fighting tactics. He was Lieutenant James McCudden, who had already built up a formidable score of 'kills' over France.

It was McCudden who first detected the problem with Mannock and discovered that in fact he was totally blind in one eye. He had spotted it during shooting practice and Mannock had to admit to the defect. But far from being tempted to 'shop' Mannock to his commanding officer and have him grounded permanently, McCudden took him under his wing and gave him extra tuition, not only in flying but also on the shooting range. The result was that Mannock became a crack shot in the air. Had it not been for McCudden's patience with the new boy, Mannock might never have achieved the fame that was ultimately to be his.

In March of 1917, Mick Mannock was presented with his wings. He had achieved what he had been waiting for and now all he wanted to do was get into action in France. Soon he was posted to a squadron near St. Omer in Northern France. At last his war was about to begin....

In France, Mannock joined No. 40 Squadron, R.F.C., one of the finest in the battle area but because of his ingrained shyness he did not immediately 'hit it off' with his fellow officers and it was to be some time before he did.

Although the war raged all around him, it was two months before Mannock got his first 'kill' and that was a German observation balloon. His superiors were not at first very impressed by his behaviour in battle. He tended to show himself unduly cautious in the air and this resulted in him gaining the nickname of 'Windy' Mannock. The truth of the matter was that Mannock was somewhat bewildered by the confusion of dog-fights when he became involved in them. He preferred to stalk or hunt his prey and attack from a position of advantage rather than get involved in the *melée* where accurate shooting was well nigh impossible. The tactics of the dogfight, he maintained, were utterly wrong and he did not hesitate to air his views on the subject. For someone who had not a single German aircraft to his credit, he was treading on shaky ground. Many felt that he ought to prove his theories in battle before expounding them to all and sundry in the mess, and this attitude brought about an even greater hostility towards him among his comrades. But Mannock was a man resolute in his purpose, hard to shake, and determined to prove himself right, in spite of all his fellows said or thought of him.

He set out to study the tactics employed by Allied and enemy pilots alike, discovering their weaknesses and their strong points, learning from them and putting their ideas into practice. As a result of this he evolved a technique which was to have devastating results. His golden rule was to attack in strength; never alone as Ball had done. He became a calculating fighter and soon his technique began to take its toll. In the first nine months of his stay in France, he shot down six German aeroplanes, was awarded the Military Cross and Bar and above all gradually gained the unflinching respect of his fellow pilots.

He perfected the technique of deflection shooting where

instead of taking the easy target by flying behind his opponent, and shooting him from there, he chose the more difficult shot and dashed in on the enemy's flank to riddle the entire length of the machine with bullets. He aimed precisely for the enemy pilot and not as most of his fellows did, just for the machine. His intention was to kill the pilot, not merely destroy the aircraft.

Such was the measure of his success that he was promoted to flight commander and this gave him fresh opportunities of fighting the way he wanted, leading his flight and launching his attacks the way he had planned. Unequalled as a tactician, he became a fine leader. He would take great pains to explain to the pilots who flew with him what tactics he would use and then after the fight would take his men aside and discuss the battle, pointing out what should have happened and what *had* happened. As a direct result of this, his men held him in high regard, some claiming that he was the finest fighter pilot in the R.F.C.

Mannock had no time for the demonstrative pilot. He thought that, while the ability to perform aerobatics was essential to a pilot's training, they were of no use whatsoever in battle. Fancy flying was not for him....or *his* pilots. It is said that on one occasion, he actually shot over the top of one of his own aircraft, loosing off a dozen or so rounds when a pilot failed to carry out his instructions to the letter. He did not believe in individualism in the air. There was only one way to fight effectively and that was as a team with each man knowing the plan of attack and sticking to it.

With constant practice he became a master of the art of stalking his prey and setting his flight up in ambush, ready to pounce when the time was right, and he spent hours ramming home his technique to his pilots. In particular he concentrated on teaching new pilots who had just arrived at his squadron and worked tirelessly on licking them into shape. His simple, golden (if not very grammatical!) rule rang in their ears every time they went into battle, — the plan for attack was always the same; *always above, seldom on the same level, never underneath.* These words formed the basis of his highly successful technique.

The fighting instinct in Mannock drove him on and his hatred for the Germans heightened when, on a number of occasions, he had to pass through areas which had been shelled or where fierce battles had taken place. There he saw at first hand the real horror of war and the enormous slaughter in which it resulted. There were to be no half measures for him. He was out to kill as many Germans as he could and would employ every means at his disposal to do so.

Once when he had shot a German two-seater he saw it crash-land in a field. He realised that the pilot and observer were still alive so he dived down on the defenceless wrecked aircraft and set about riddling it with machine-gun bullets until both the occupants lay motionless. Such was Mannock's hatred for the enemy. For him there was none of the friendly camaraderie of the air. The duelling spirit was not for Mannock. Unlike many other pilots on both sides. he showed not the slightest hint of respect for his enemy. He wanted as many as possible of them dead and buried.

This ruthless attitude of Mannock's was best illustrated when, one day, he returned to the squadron mess to hear the news that Baron Manfred von Richthofen had been killed. When someone proposed a toast to the memory of that great German ace, Mannock marched resolutely out of the mess in disgust, mouthing oaths as he went. His only regret was that it had not been he who had shot down Richthofen!

In spite of this hard exterior, Mannock had his own inner fears to face. As his score of kills dramatically rose, he witnessed more and more German and British aircraft plunging to the ground in flames. The very sight of such a horrible death sickened him and he was constantly aware that he too might one day suffer such a fate. Even his dreams were tortured by the thought of such a terrible ending and he would wake up at night in a cold sweat having relived the death of one of his opponents or dreamt that he was, himself, in a burning aircraft and unable to get out. As time went on, this fear grew in intensity but it did not prevent him from pressing home his attacks with the same determination. He became a fatalist, knowing that one day he too, like so many of his comrades, would perish, but determined that before he went he would kill as many Germans as possible. For this reason he went to great lengths and often took needless risks to ensure that his opponents had really been destroyed, following them right down until they hit the ground.

Mannock's score of victories soon topped fifty and he was admitted to the Distinguished Service Order but he had little time for medals even when a short time later he was awarded a Bar to that D.S.O. The only significance medals had for him was as indications of the number of his kills in the air.

But now the strain of continual fighting was beginning to tell on Mannock's nerves. He flew almost daily on missions over enemy territory, dicing with death all the time and the tension of such a strenuous life was beginning to have an effect on him. Others noticed this and eventually he was sent home to England with strict instructions to take a rest before returning. Reluctantly he left, but not before having a final crack at the enemy only hours before his departure.

After a brief rest, Mannock learned to his horror that he had been posted to a training unit in England where he was to teach untrained pilots the art of air combat. Furious, he demanded to be sent back to France. At first his demands were refused; the high command claiming that he was of greater use training young men to go into battle than risking his own life in the air. But Mannock was adamant and made such a nuisance of himself that the authorities relented and allowed him to return, promoting him to major and giving him command of his own squadron.

Mannock was, on the one hand, delighted at the news of his promotion and new command but heartbroken at having to leave his old squadron where he had spent so long and made so many loyal and trusted friends. Shortly afterwards, the stunning news reached him that his friend and former teacher, James McCudden had been killed while taking off on a mission. It is said that upon hearing the news, Mannock wept.

Once he had overcome the initial shock of his friend's death, Mannock was fired with an even greater resolve for revenge. At all costs he would avenge the death of McCudden and he went about it with unequalled ferocity. His score rocketed into the sixties and he delighted in the thought that each victory was another toll exacted for McCudden.

Then came the day when his score entered the seventies and he caught up with the reigning champion, Major 'Billy' Bishop who had a score of seventy-two. It now became obsessional with Mannock that he should get one more 'kill' to become the supreme ace of aces. But it was about this time that he got his strongest-ever premonition of death, one that he could not hide from his closest friends. It was to his friend 'Taffy' Jones, a flight commander, that he one day confessed....

'I'm just like any other pilot. I'm scared stiff when I see my Hun floating down in flames.'

Taffy could see that Mannock was deeply depressed but while they were talking, they were joined by one of the 'new boys' of the squadron, Lieutenant Inglis, a young New Zealander who had yet to bring down an enemy aircraft. As if trying to snap himself out of his depression, Mannock turned to Inglis and said....

'Have you got yourself a Hun yet, Kiwi?'

'No, sir,' Inglis replied in a quiet voice, almost too afraid to admit it.

'Then come on, lad,' Mannock said rising from his seat. 'We'd better see what we can do about that, eh?'

Inglis rose and followed Mannock out of the mess towards two parked aircraft. Mannock was the first into his cockpit with his engine revving into life, but Inglis found he had trouble with one of his elevators and could not take off. Not noticing this, Mannock was airborne before he realised that he was alone. He pressed on alone but found no enemy planes, so he returned to base.

Inglis was disappointed, but Mannock quickly reassured him by offering to take him up the following morning before dawn. With a parting warning to Inglis to make sure his machine was serviceable for the morning, Mannock strode off to the officers' mess and there met up with Taffy once more. The Welshman continued to question Mannock about his depression.

'I don't think I'm going to last much longer, Taffy,' Mannock told him. 'You watch yourself. Don't go following any Huns too low or you will end up joining the "sizzle-brigade" with me.'

The following morning Mannock entered a deserted mess and waited for Inglis. His mind was troubled and he was obviously deep in thought when Inglis finally arrived.

'Come on, Kiwi,' he said. 'We'll get up there and see if we can find you a nice two-seater to bang away at.'

As they made their way out to the waiting aircraft which had already been warmed up by the mechanics, Mannock gave Inglis his final instructions....

'Now don't forget – keep close to my tail and follow my

movements. If you're too far behind, I'll waggle my wings, Okay?'

When he arrived at his aircraft, Mannock did something he had never done before. He shook hands with all his mechanics as if in farewell. Then, as he climbed into the cockpit, one of them wished him success in getting his seventy-third Hun. With the roar of the two aircraft breaking the morning stillness, they took off and soon disappeared in the direction of enemy territory.

Inglis did as his leader had instructed. He kept on his tail, giving little bursts of speed when Mannock waggled his wings. Then suddenly, without warning, Mannock banked sharply with his guns blazing. For a moment, Inglis wondered what had happened then he saw it....right in front of him was a plump L.V.G. German aircraft already riddled with holes from Mannock's guns. Inglis steadied his aircraft then fired a long burst which sent the aircraft tumbling earthwards with flames licking out of it.

Mannock, having achieved his seventy-third victory. followed the German down, flying circles round the great torch of flame, watched from above by Inglis. Then Inglis noticed something odd. Mannock's plane quite suddenly seemed to go out of control and lapse into a right-hand bank. Inglis watched amazed until he saw the faint flicker of flame lick out of the right-hand side of the aircraft. The flames spread rapidly. Soon the whole aircraft was a raging furnace as it screeched towards the ground. Seconds later it hit and exploded in a great ball of fire.

Inglis was not to know it then but Mannock's aircraft had been riddled from stem to stern by machine-gun fire from the ground. The ace of aces was dead.

Unable to believe what he had seen, Inglis swept low over the burning wreckage then turned his machine homewards. But he had no sooner done so than he too was hit, though he succeeded in limping away to land his machine behind the Allied lines, where British tommies rushed over to him. They found him sitting in his cockpit sobbing, and muttering over and over again, the same words...

'They've shot my major down....'

In spite of an intensive search, no trace was ever found of Mannock's machine or his body. Jim Eyles continued the search well after the end of the war but it was in vain.

Major Edward 'Mick' Mannock D.S.O. and Bar, M.C. and Bar, the most successful fighter pilot the R.A.F. had ever had, died in the way he feared most of all....in flames. His terrible premonition had come true.

Had Mannock lived he would have seen, in only four months, the downfall and defeat of the race he hated so much, for the war came to an end on the 11th of November 1918. The following year, Major Mannock was posthumously awarded the country's highest award for valour, the Victoria Cross.

The citation read:

'For bravery of the highest order....This highly distinguished officer, during the whole of his career in the Royal Air Force, was an outstanding example of fearless courage, remarkable skill, devotion to duty and self sacrifice, which has never been surpassed.'

5
Zeppelin Attack

One cold, dark evening in 1912, an incident took place which was to shake the peace of Britain and send a scare throughout the length and breadth of the country.

That night, the seaside town of Sheerness lay shrouded in darkness; the black cloak of night pierced only by a few dim lights glowing from behind closed curtains. Few souls ventured out that night to brave the icy blast of winter and all lay still and peaceful until, suddenly, the winter silence was broken by the sound of engines coming from the direction of the sea. The drone of the engines was not the familiar chugging of a trawler returning from the fishing grounds. No, this was something quite different and the sound appeared to be coming from the darkness overhead.

As the noise of engines grew louder, a small crowd gathered by the water's edge. It could only be an aircraft, they all agreed. But for an aircraft to pass over there was a rare enough event during the day and at night it was unheard of.

Idle curiosity brought more people to the water's edge. Then suddenly, a shout came from amid the group.

'There it is, over there!' shouted a man, pointing his finger into the sky.

Heads turned and eyes strained. High above the dark rolling waves of the North Sea was a light, piercing the inky blackness.

'That's a bloomin' star,' another man said contemptuously.

'That's no star, mate,' said another. 'There's no star that moves through the sky like that.'

A hush fell over the crowd. Sure enough the light was moving. As they watched, it glided slowly across the sky then faded and disappeared, enveloped in the cloak of darkness. With it went the noise of the engines and immediately the crowd broke into a babble of excited chatter.

'What could it have been?' one man asked eagerly.

'Search me,' answered his neighbour. 'Reckon it must've been one of these new-fangled flying machines....or maybe one of these airships we've been reading so much about in the papers.'

'I don't like it,' remarked his companion warily. 'Supposin' it is an airship, what's it doing sneaking around here at night, eh?'

Word of the sighting soon reached the newspapers and reports of this strange occurrence spread through the country like wild-fire. Soon sense and reason gave away to wild speculation and rumours of all sorts of impending disasters were rife throughout the country, even whispers of an invasion by a foreign power were not uncommon.

The people of Britain wanted to know what it was that had lurked near their coast then slipped stealthily off into the night. Questions were asked in the House of Commons and a full-scale investigation called for.

The Royal Navy was in those days responsible for home defence and the Admiralty lost no time in getting to work. Naval Intelligence swung into action and the navy's 'cloak and dagger' men combed Europe for the answer, tapping every possible source of information. Eventually it came.

The British public was stunned when Winston Churchill, then the First Lord of the Admiralty, announced that the lights seen off the coast had been those of an airship, but that it had not been one of ours. Intelligence sources proved beyond the shadow of a doubt that the airship came from Germany.

When the newspapers carried banner headlines proclaiming the truth, Britain was in an uproar. One burning question was uppermost in the minds of the British people. Why had a German airship paid a clandestine visit to the shores of England? In only two years they were to find out.

The gigantic Zeppelin airship was the brain-child of the German Count von Zeppelin from whom it took its name. He had first flown a Zeppelin just before the turn of the century and had met with great success. The enormous airships were around 500 feet in length and resembled huge canvas-covered flying cigars filled with hydrogen gas. Slung beneath these vast cigars were gondolas which housed the crew of sixteen. The lighter-than-air hydrogen gas gave the airship its lift and the engines its forward thrust.

Inspired by the success of the first experimental airship, von Zeppelin built more and was quick to see that his airships could be used successfully as weapons of war. They could cruise with ease at heights around 10,000 feet, well out of the accurate range of enemy anti-aircraft guns. He carried out a whole series of tests, dropping bombs from a Zeppelin on practice targets in Germany. The bombing was far from accurate but the count foresaw the terrifying psychological effects aerial bombardment would have upon an enemy.

Throughout 1913, anxiety grew to fever pitch in Britain as more mysterious lights were sighted at night off the south-west coast and news of Count Zeppelin's bombing trials reached England. Worried politicians soon put two and two together. The Zeppelins had already proved that they could reach England. What then if they carried a load of bombs and began an aerial bombardment of our cities? Relations between Britain and Germany were strained almost to breaking point and the possibility of war now began to seem very real. If war came, what defence would Britain have against these monsters in the sky? The answer was terrifyingly simple — none!

The Royal Flying Corps was little more than a year old and had only a handful of primitive aircraft which would take almost an hour to reach the operational height of an attacking Zeppelin. The Royal Navy was not much better off. A few guns were placed at strategic points along the south

coast but they were wildly inaccurate when firing at a target
10,000 feet in the air – and the Zeppelins might not come
that way.

Worse still was the fact that argument raged between the
Navy and the Royal Flying Corps as to whose responsibility
it was to defend the country in the event of war. Each
claimed that this task was the other's responsibility. As long
as this inter-service squabble continued the defence situation
could obviously grow no better. In consequence when war
was declared in August 1914, the country was still almost
completely defenceless against aerial attack. The Royal
Flying Corps' best machines and pilots were very soon sent to
France, leaving behind only a skeleton force, and the Navy
had its permanent commitments at sea. But one swift, deadly
blow was soon to come which was to stir the defence chiefs
into taking positive action.

On December 21st, 1914, a lone German seaplane droned
across the English Channel and dropped a stick of bombs into
the sea near Dover. Although the bombs exploded harmlessly
in the sea, the Germans' intentions were clear. Aerial attacks
on Britain were imminent. Then on Christmas Day another
attack was made, this time with greater effect. Two bombs
were dropped on Dover and exploded, damaging a few
houses. Luckily no one was killed.

The Royal Navy was given strict instructions to take
immediate action to combat the new bombing menace. More
anti-aircraft guns and batteries of high-powered searchlights
were hurriedly moved into position at points along the coast.
Their gunners manned their guns and waited....

Night after night and day after day they waited. Days
passed into months, but still there was no sign of the much
talked of Zeppelin invasion. Then in May 1915, after months
of agonising waiting, it came.

Over several towns on the south and east coasts of England
the ominous drone of engines was heard, quickly followed by
ear-piercing high-pitched whistles as hundreds of pounds of
incendiaries and high-explosive bombs hurtled earthwards to
explode with a deafening roar. Most of the bombs fell far off
target and did little or no damage but the effect on the
British population was shattering. This was something people
had not bargained for. They were completely exposed and
yet helpless to retaliate in any way.

The Zeppelin captains could safely scoff at Britain's puny attempts to defend herself, laughing contemptuously as the Navy's anti-aircraft shells burst far below them. There was no early warning system in those days to alert pilots of an impending attack. The result was that, when the call to action came, the Zeppelins had already reached their targets, dropped their bombs and were on their way home. Even on the very rare occasions when an aircraft did manage to get within range and fire a burst of bullets at the huge gas-filled hulks, the pilots had the frustrating experience of watching their tracer bullets rip through the canvas and out the other side without doing any harm. All they succeeded in doing was puncturing the canvas and allowing some gas to escape but this had little or no effect on the airship's performance. The mighty German Zeppelin fleet could bomb England with impunity.

On the night of 31st May 1915, the Zeppelin captains, flushed with the success of their previous raids, turned their attentions to what was for them the most tempting target of all, London. That night high-explosive and incendiary bombs rained savagely down on the city, exploding amongst the closely built houses. Buildings were demolished in seconds, as bombs thudded into them ripping them apart. Fires raged and terrified Londoners fled through the streets in a blind panic. Miraculously only seven people were killed and less than forty injured.

Compared with the German blitz on London during the Second World War, this Zeppelin raid was a mere flash in the pan. But it must be remembered that London had never suffered anything like it before. The startling element of surprise was enough to panic the stoutest person. Germany's savage attack on innocent civilians made British blood boil. The British people wanted revenge and they wanted it quickly. What infuriated them most was the thought that not one of the Zeppelins had suffered the slightest damage.

London was in turmoil. Urgent warnings were given by the police to the public to remain calm and stay indoors during raids. Londoners slept uneasily in their beds, waiting for the ominous drone of the Zeppelins. Fear spread through the city like wild-fire when rumours became rife that the Germans planned to use mustard gas bombs.

Scientists worked day and night in a frantic bid to devise a weapon which could be used effectively against the Zeppelins. One invention was a small fire-bomb which the scientists hopefully thought could be dropped on a Zeppelin from above and explode on contact. The idea was ingenious but it had one distinct drawback. The aircraft had first to get above the Zeppelin before it could launch its attack and with the type of slow, cumbersome aeroplane used by the R.F.C. and the Royal Naval Air Service, this was almost impossible. The successful use of this fire-bomb depended entirely upon the attacking aircraft having the luck to be in the right place at the right time. Very early on the morning of June 7th, 1915, that vital stroke of luck came.

Flight Sub-Lieutenant Warneford, of the Royal Naval Air Service, had been a fully-qualified pilot for only three months when, flying his small two-seater Morane monoplane on patrol between Brussels and Ghent, in Belgium, he saw the huge, dark shape of a Zeppelin nosing its way through the night sky. A chance in a thousand had presented itself and Warneford wasn't going to lose it. He rammed forward his throttle and pulled back on the control column, lifting the nose of his aircraft. The little Le Rhône engine moaned as it strained to pull the Morane upwards. The icy wind whipped into Warneford's face as the monoplane inched higher and higher. The suspense was agonising, as gradually the mighty Zeppelin loomed larger and larger ahead of him. At last he was above the massive cigar-shaped airship and hurriedly he prepared to release his six anti-Zeppelin bombs.

'Must take my time,' he told himself. 'Mustn't miss.'

He was tempted to throw the bombs out and hope that one would find the target but he fought against this senseless urge and waited. Seconds later he was directly over the great black shadow.

'Now!' he thought.

One by one his six bombs shot downwards towards the airship. In an instant there was a blinding flash as the fire-bombs ignited the gas and the sky was ablaze with light. The explosion caught Warneford's aircraft and tossed it upside down. The flaming inferno roared below him as he fought with the controls to right the aircraft. But the searing heat blew him higher above the holocaust of fire.

Summoning all his strength, he rammed the stick over to the side and rolled over, flying straight and level once more.

Now he could look down upon the fruits of his efforts. He saw the great fireball tilt slowly then gently slide towards the ground. At last a Zeppelin had fallen to a British attacker. Warneford had shattered the invincibility of this sinister weapon.

He began to shout with joy but his jubilation was cut short when his engine spluttered and cut out. Instantly the nose of the Morane dropped and the monoplane began to glide towards the ground. Down she floated, while Warneford strained his eyes to find a suitable place to make a landing.

Flying at night in those days was no easy task. It required very real ability and courage. With no artificial horizon instrument to tell Warneford whether or not he was flying straight and level, he had to rely entirely upon sighting lights on the ground. But at that time Warneford had more light than he wanted. The blinding glow from the burning airship was dazzlingly bright. However, whether he could see clearly or not, he had to land. Gingerly he touched down on a rough piece of ground and rumbled to a halt.

Warneford leapt out of his cockpit and feverishly got to work on the engine. He had to work fast because he had landed behind the enemy lines and he realised that soon the whole area would be swarming with troops. They would certainly not take kindly to the pilot who had shot down one of their precious airships. The seconds ticked by as he tinkered with the engine. Then at last it burst into life and Warneford took off. With a final look at the blazing airship, he headed for his base.

Warneford arrived at his base to a hero's welcome and news of his success was flashed to Britain where it brought fresh hope to the nation. He was a national hero overnight and for his bravery he was later awarded the Victoria Cross.

At last spirits began to rise in Britain but one all-important issue could not be avoided. Warneford had attacked the airship at 6000 feet which was far below the Zeppelin's normal operating height. Furthermore, he had been airborne when he made contact with the Zeppelin, unlike his fellow pilots at home who had the disadvantage of having to rely on very short warning when a Zeppelin was approaching to attack. Could his success be copied by others, in view of these facts?

It was obvious that drastic re-organisation of the defence

system in Britain was needed before pilots had even an outside chance of doing so.

The defence chiefs put their heads together and came up with what seemed like a reasonable answer. A ring of anti-aircraft guns, together with searchlight batteries was set up around London. In addition, the R.F.C. operating from airfields around the Metropolis, was to maintain continuous airborne patrols along Zeppelin routes throughout every night, using their crack pilots for the job. This meant that aircraft would be in the air and waiting for the Zeppelins when they made their attack.

A black-out system was introduced to make both navigation and accurate bombing more difficult for the Zeppelin captains and, perhaps more important, an early warning system was devised. Special lookouts were posted at points along the usual Zeppelin routes. These men, who kept a nightly watch on the skies, each had a direct telephone link with their headquarters. When an enemy airship was sighted, the observer would telephone his headquarters which would in turn alert the R.F.C. and the anti-aircraft gunners of the impending attack. The system *seemed* foolproof.

Britain waited for news of the first Zeppelin 'kill' over England but she was to wait a long time. The airships kept coming, penetrating the new defence system, slipping through the night and with ruthless determination keeping up their reign of terror. Try as they might the R.F.C. pilots seemed unable to deliver that crushing blow that would find the Achilles Heel of the Zeppelin fleet. The frustration felt by the British pilots was enormous.

One pilot, Lieutenant John Slessor (later to become Marshal of the R.A.F., Sir John Slessor) was alerted one night in October that a Zeppelin had crossed the English coast. Dashing to his waiting aircraft he jumped into the cockpit, taking off and climbing as fast as he could in the direction of the oncoming Zeppelin. But as had happened so often in the past, by the time he had caught sight of the Zeppelin, it had already dropped its bombs on London. However, Slessor was determined not to let this one go. He roared in on the airship but the Zeppelin's captain heard the oncoming engine and at full throttle headed off into the night. Slessor, furious, had no choice but to let it go. He hadn't a chance of catching up on it. Dejected he headed back to base.

Navigation at night was tricky and was made doubly difficult by the newly-enforced blackout in Britain. Slessor, however, was a skilled pilot and soon spotted the crude flarepath which had been lit along the runway. Flying almost 'by the seat of his pants' he eased the aircraft gently down towards the black ground between the two rows of flame. Just then, to his horror, the lights became hazy as a blanket of fog rolled over them.

On the ground, the crew of a searchlight battery saw Slessor's predicament and switched on their brilliant light to illuminate the grass. But instead of helping Slessor, they almost blinded him, with the dazzling light reflected off the fog making the ground a glowing white. Only Slessor's supreme skill as a pilot saved him from a horrible death. As it was, his frail little craft was only slightly damaged in the landing. Through no fault on the part of the pilot, another Zeppelin had slipped through the net to raid again another day.

As the months passed, more pilots succeeded in making contact with Zeppelins but to their bitter disappointment, none of them managed to make a 'kill'. Time after time, they would get well within striking distance and pump hundreds of machine-gun bullets into the massive hulks but without result.

Another difficulty when attacking a high-flying Zeppelin was the lack of oxygen at 10,000 feet. Aircraft in those days were not fitted with oxygen tanks and the rarefied atmosphere played funny tricks on pilots. Often they would lapse into a drunken-like state and become light-headed, losing control of their aircraft which would career about the sky before finally plunging to the ground. The R.F.C. lost more than one pilot in this way.

The open cockpit, also, afforded little protection against the elements and frost-bite was an ever-present hazard. Even on a hot summer day, flying in an open cockpit was a chilly experience but in the middle of the night despite fur-lined gloves and layers of extra clothing, it was bitterly cold.

Yet in spite of the many dangers they had to face, these brave men continued to fly their nightly patrols, each determined to become the first man to bring down a Zeppelin over British soil. In Germany, meanwhile, the Zeppelin crews continued to boast arrogantly of their mastery of the air over Britain. But a young R.F.C. lieutenant was soon to change the picture.

On the evening of September 2nd, 1916, the mighty German airship S.L.11 rose into the air from its base in Belgium along with fifteen others. The armada of Zeppelins climbed higher and set course for England.

Captain Wilhelm Schramm, commander of the S.L.11 stood proudly at the window of the command cabin looking out into the night sky. In the airship's bomb-bay nestled a ton of high-explosive bombs for their target....London. The sixteen man crew of the S.L.11 was in good spirits. Once more they were on their way to strike another blow for the glorious fatherland.

Schramm turned and paced purposefully up and down the cabin, pausing only occasionally to snap an order to the helmsman to change course. He felt confident that this would be yet another successful raid on the British capital. He and his crew had raided London many times before and returned unscathed. There was little for them to fear, he thought.

By eleven o'clock that evening the airship was slipping across the English coast and Schramm watched as the luminescent sea changed to the dark mass of land.

But far below, a pair of watchful eyes scanned the sky and caught sight of the huge black shape nosing its way inland. The eyes were those of one of the new observers. He dashed to the telephone and hurriedly warned his headquarters of the approaching enemy.

Within minutes, the warning was being passed on to the R.F.C. airfields around London and gunners manning the anti-aircraft guns around the city scrambled to their positions, ready for action.

The duty pilot at Sutton's Farm airfield that night was Lieutenant William Leefe-Robinson of the R.F.C. At a few minutes after 11 o'clock the telephone jangled into life. He answered it.

'German airship spotted crossing the coast on a heading for London. All available aircraft to be airborne for interception immediately,' the voice at the other end said excitedly.

'I'm on my way,' Leefe-Robinson said quickly and hung up.

Already clad in his flying suit, he dashed out onto the airfield, shouting to his ground crew to follow. Mechanics fussed around the waiting aircraft while Leefe-Robinson jumped into the cockpit and pulled on his flying helmet. Quickly he went through his pre-flight checks, testing the various controls and seconds later he shouted to the mechanic standing by the plane's propeller:

'Contact!'

The mechanic pulled down on the propeller blade and the engine spluttered into life.

'Chocks away!' Leefe-Robinson bawled above the noise of the engine and two men pulled away the blocks in front of the wheels. Leefe-Robinson eased forward the throttle and the frail little B.E.2c aircraft rumbled across the grass field to take-off point.

Leefe-Robinson's heart beat faster with excitement as the tiny aeroplane bumped over the uneven grass surface of the field. Then he turned her into the wind, pushed the throttle forward to full power and off she went, trundling along the grass and into the air.

The biting September wind lanced the young pilot's face and whistled through the mass of struts and wires on the delicate biplane as the small 70 hp engine strained at full power to pull the aeroplane through the air. Slowly the B.E.2c inched higher and higher into the starlit sky and Leefe-Robinson pondered on his chances of making contact with the raider.

'If only I can gain height in time, I'll have a fighting chance of getting a crack at one of them,' he muttered aloud.

The minutes ticked by as the aeroplane rose into the sky over Hornchurch and headed in the direction of the oncoming German airship. Far over towards London, Leefe-Robinson could see the searchlight beams already probing the sky.

An hour passed without event. By then he was flying at 12,000 feet. Then suddenly he saw a great, ghostly, silver shape coned in searchlight beams far ahead of him.

'This is it!' he thought. But no sooner had he changed direction to attack the airship than it wriggled free of the searchlights and disappeared. He cursed his bad luck and was forced to resign himself to the fact that he had missed it.

He banked his aircraft steeply and returned to his patrol area. For a further hour he flew back and forwards along a line between Hornchurch and Joyce Green. He had almost given up hope of another sighting when in an instant the searchlights were lit again. The long thin pencils of light swept across the sky, searching for an airship which had been reported in the area.

In S.L.11, Captain Schramm cursed the searchlights which probed the sky for his ship. The element of surprise was lost and now his one thought was to drop his bomb-load and make a dash for home.

'Release the bombs,' he yelled in a fury and the deadly load hurtled earthwards. Schramm peered down and watched his bombs explode amongst the houses. His job was done.

'Head for home,' he ordered. But the words had barely left his lips when the ship was bathed in light.

'Ach! They have found us!' Schramm yelled and turned to the helmsman, 'Manoeuvre, you idiot,' he barked, 'Get out of the light.'

Far below, men, women and children rushed out into the streets as the guns roared and peered into the night sky to see what was happening.

At that moment, Leefe-Robinson caught sight of the enemy, coned in the beams of half a dozen searchlights. He swung his machine in the direction of the glowing airship.

'This is one Hun who isn't going to get away!' he thought. His machine was higher than the Zeppelin and in a perfect position for an attack.

In the command cabin of the airship, Schramm was yelling frantic orders to his crew. The mighty airship weaved about the sky in a bid to dodge the searchlights but could not throw them off.

Leefe-Robinson shot down towards the airship with the wind catching his breath. His gloved fore-finger curled round the trigger of his Lewis gun. He had three drums of incendiary and tracer bullets.

'Every bullet must count,' he muttered to himself.

By then a furious barrage of shells was exploding around the airship but, unconcerned, Leefe-Robinson flew straight into the wall of fire.

He dived alongside the huge hulk and squeezed the trigger of his Lewis guns, spraying the length of the ship with bullets. Nothing happened. He watched in a fury as the tracer bullets passed harmlessly through the massive gas bags.

Quickly he changed drums on his machine-gun and attacked once more but again the bullets had no effect on the airship.

With blind determination driving him on, he dived underneath the rear of the airship and pulled up. As he clamped on his last drum of ammunition the small plane was tossed about the sky by the blast from exploding shells. Bits of shrapnel slashed the canvas covering the fuselage of his plane but he raced on. Completely disregarding the flak, he set his sights on the belly of the ship and squeezed the trigger. A hail of explosive bullets spat from his machine-gun and raked the bottom of the airship. Suddenly the whole tail end of the airship glowed in a diffused red. Then the glow grew in intensity along the length of the airship. Leefe-Robinson's heart missed a beat. The whole world seemed to stop for a fraction of a second then a flash shot out of the mighty hulk and it burst into a gigantic flaming inferno. It seemed as if the heavens were ablaze as the airship hung for a moment in the sky then dropped its nose towards the ground.

The enormous ball of fire was hurtling down on top of Leefe-Robinson's aircraft. He rammed the stick over and shot out of its way. As it plunged past him the deafening roar of the raging fire reached his ears and the intense heat scorched his face.

Like a huge roman candle, the blazing airship slipped towards the ground and crumpled into the earth with a thundering crash near Cuffley, not far from Enfield.

It was only then that Leefe-Robinson realised what he had achieved. Elated at his victory, he zoomed over the burning wreckage, firing red Very lights and dropping parachute flares. The first German airship ever to be brought down over British soil had fallen to his guns. Singing with joy, he headed for home.

The following day, the whole nation knew of the young pilot's success when the late editions of the newspapers carried banner headlines proclaiming Leefe-Robinson a hero. Hundred of thousands of Londoners had witnessed the death of the airship from the streets and were overcome with joy.

For his courage, Lieutenant Leefe-Robinson was awarded the Victoria Cross. His success that night gave the British people the shot in the arm they so desperately needed and morale rose.

But in the German capital the fate of the S.L.11 had dealt a shattering blow to the Zeppelin crews. No longer could they fly over England without fear of attack. It needed little imagination to realise the horrible death Captain Schramm and his crew had suffered. The fear of a similar fate bit into the hearts of the Zeppelin commanders and their crews but the German High Command was adamant that the raids must continue. They thought that the R.F.C. had just been lucky. But if luck it had been, then that luck was to stay with the R.F.C....

The Germans were out for revenge and another terror raid was planned for a night late in September. This time eleven airships took off from the continent and set course for England. But now the crews sat grim-faced at the controls. They were on edge and wary of what lay in store for them over England.

Among the force of Zeppelins that night was the L.33, commanded by Captain Boeker, a seasoned veteran of the Zeppelin raids. He, unlike his comrades, was not put off by Leefe-Robinson's success. He headed for London while most of the other Zeppelins made for the easier, less well defended targets.

But once over London, Boeker's airship was almost immediately caught in searchlights and he hurriedly dropped his bombs. Just then the rattle of machine-gun fire sent him dashing to one of the windows. Peering out he could see a British aircraft bearing down on the airship and raking it with fire.

The aircraft, a B.E.2c was flown by Lieutenant Brandon. He circled the ship, lashing it with fire until he had exhausted all his ammunition but nothing happened and he was forced to break off his attack. Disheartened he returned to base.

But Brandon need not have been downhearted. His bullets had peppered the Zeppelin's gas bags with holes and the hydrogen gas was escaping fast.

Boeker cursed the British pilot as the airship gradually lost height. He squeezed every ounce of power he could get out of the Zeppelin's engines but it soon became obvious to him that he would not be able to get back to the continent. Then he ordered his crew to throw everything they could out of the ship in a bid to lessen the weight and maintain height. But it was all to no avail. The ship continued to lose height.

As it neared the English coast, one of the crew gazed horror-struck as he spotted flames licking out of the canvas. This was the end. Boeker gave the order to land and the airship touched down in a field. The crew was saved and spent the remainder of the war as prisoners.

Boeker and his crew were lucky. They were at least alive but another crew was not so lucky that night. They were to perish in a fiery hell. Their airship fell to the guns of Lieutenant Sowrey, who chased the Zeppelin L.32 across the sky and riddled it with tracer bullets until it exploded and crashed to the ground.

That September night dealt the decisive blow to the Germans. None of the commanders would, thereafter, dare carry out a raid on London. None, that is, except one....the most famous Zeppelin commander of them all, Captain Mathy.

On a night early in October 1916, Mathy's Zeppelin raided London, dropping its load of bombs, but hardly had she done so than she was bathed in light. The master commander had been caught.

Lieutenant Tempest, flying his B.E.2c, spotted the tell-tale glow not far away from where he was flying on patrol. Without hesitation, he dived to the attack and unleashed a hail of fire. His bullets thudded into the huge gas bags and Tempest gazed, awe-struck, as the mighty Zeppelin burst into flames and toppled towards the ground.

The greatest of all the Zeppelin commanders was dead. The blow to German morale was such that London was never again attacked by Zeppelins. The menace had been thwarted once and for all.

6
The Death of an Airship

Long before Orville and Wilbur Wright made their first successful flight in a powered, fixed-wing aircraft, great strides had been made in the development of another form of air transport – the airship.

Although there were a great many variations of design, an airship was essentially a huge fabric-covered envelope containing a vast quantity of lighter-than-air gas (generally hydrogen) which enabled it to rise from the ground and gave it its upward lift. Obviously an airship was of little use if it could travel only upwards and remain at the mercy of the prevailing winds (like a balloon), so to give it forward thrust, propellers, driven by engines, were fitted onto gondolas or pylons slung beneath the great envelope of gas.

It fell to a Frenchman, Henri Giffard, to build and fly the first successful airship. He made an enormous bag which he filled with gas and beneath which he suspended a gondola, which not only housed the pilot but also the 3 horse-power steam engine which drove the propeller. One day in 1852, he made the first-ever airship flight when he took off from Paris and flew to Trappes. Giffard's machine however, had a top speed of only 6 miles an hour and was found to be virtually uncontrollable.

The real turning point in airship aviation came in 1898 when a Brazilian, called Santos Dumont, married the airship to the petrol engine. His airship was what is known as non-rigid; that is, it relied upon the gas inside it to keep its shape. In 1901 he won a 125,000 franc prize when he flew his airship from Saint Cloud, in France, round the Eiffel Tower in Paris, and back in only thirty minutes.

But the man who above all others did most to improve and develop the airship was the German Count Ferdinand von Zeppelin. His construction differed from the others in that it had a rigid, covered framework inside which were hollow compartments filled with gas. In 1910, he began the first ever regular air passenger service which plied between Lake Constance and Berlin as well as other German cities. Before the outbreak of the First World War, his Zeppelins had carried more than 35,000 passengers, and you have already read how they performed in their missions over Britain carrying out the first Blitz of London.

After the war, the Germans built the mighty Graf Zeppelin and the Hindenburg both of which made transatlantic flights to America. These giants of the sky were truly remarkable constructions with spacious and luxurious accommodation for their passengers, such as has not been matched since. Their public rooms resembled those of luxury liners and indeed were designed to compete with them.

The popularity of the airship as a means of comparatively fast travel grew in the 1920s and those devotees of this form of transport reckoned it was the most efficient way of carrying passengers over long distances. It had its rival, though, in the shape of the flying boat, but still it seemed to out-do the aeroplane at every turn. In 1929 the Graf Zeppelin made a spectacular 21,500 mile round-the-world trip in only three weeks, flying the 7000 mile stage from Friedrichshafen, in Germany, to Tokyo, Japan, *non-stop*.

The Germans, however, were not alone in developing the airship. The British had been hard at work experimenting at the Royal Aircraft Establishment at Farnborough. In 1919 the British R.34 became the first airship to cross the Atlantic both ways, taking 108 hours to complete the east-west journey. Eventually came the R.100, built by the Vickers Aircraft Company, which made a successful flight from Scotland to Canada and back. That was in July 1930, but less than two months later disaster was to strike the British airship industry....

For six years workers laboured on the construction of the R.101, the sister ship of the R.100, which was being built by the Airship Guarantee Company Ltd., a government sponsored concern. It was envisaged that this flying behemoth would one day fly to India via Egypt in no more than 74 hours (carrying upwards of 130 passengers) a truly remarkable saving in time on the normal ocean-liner time of 17 days.

Throughout the period of her construction, the British public was kept informed of her progress by masses of features and articles in the press. A virtual airship mania existed in the British newspapers and magazines and the man who headed the design and construction team, Colonel V.C. Richmond, was in the news almost continuously. Although he had had no previous experience of airship design, he had proved himself an expert with considerable experience in other fields of aviation. He and his team of designers ranked amongst the most knowledgeable in the country.

The construction of the mighty R.101 took place in a vast shed which still exists today at Cardington, near Bedford. The airship was to be 724 feet long, almost double the size of any existing airship at that time, and it was to be powered by no less than five engines. The accommodation provided for the passengers was to be the last word in luxury, giving the appearance of an exclusive hotel. There would be a smoking room complete with an aluminium floor as a guard against fire. There would be a crew of forty-eight to fly the airship and cater for every need of the passengers. There was to be a chart room and a separate control room from which the airship would be flown. The R.101 was, it seemed, a model of design and luxury. But although the plans for her seemed well nigh perfect, the actual construction was running far from smoothly.

It was originally planned that the R.101 would be ready for flight testing in 1927 but as early as the year before, it had become obvious that she was running far behind schedule. Innumerable problems had been encountered, not the least of which concerned the giant propellers on the Beardmore engines. During one of the tests on an engine specially rigged up at Cardington, the propellers had disintegrated into a thousand pieces, scattering jagged metal with razor sharp edges round a wide area. Fortunately, the chief engineer had had the sense to erect a protective shield which saved him and his mechanics from being cut to ribbons by the flying metal. Further investigations showed that the propellers had suffered metal fatigue at the roots. The propeller blades were just not strong enough for the engines. After more tests, the engineers succeeded in arriving at a solution to the problem by securing the blades in place using high-tensile steel bolts.

By then vast sums of money had already been spent on the construction of the airship, far more than the original budget had allowed for and the builders were subjected to considerable pressure from the government to get the ship completed quickly and into operation.

At last, after hurried modifications and alterations had been made to the R.101, she was ready for her test flights. She made them but there was almost continuous trouble with the 'pusher' engines which powered the ship. The method of overcoming these problems was crude to say the least and had more time been available perhaps a more satisfactory and reliable solution could have been found. As it was the results were far from satisfactory. Indeed more than one person voiced the opinion that all was not well with the design of the craft.

In 1929, the R.101 went on her first long test flight, which lasted some thirty hours, after which it was obvious that she required more really dramatic changes. She had failed miserably to meet the specified 'lift' requirements; she was sluggish in gaining height, a fault that could not be tolerated. Back she went into her shed in Cardington where she was sliced in half and lengthened by 53 feet to accommodate more hydrogen gas bags. This, the designers hoped, would provide the extra lift they needed.

The alteration had caused a considerable delay in finishing the airship and pressure was mounting at an even greater rate to finish her quickly. Perhaps the most important cause for haste was the necessity to prove the success of the airship before an Imperial Conference on Air Transport which was due to be held on October 20th, 1930. It went without saying that if the R.101 failed to make a successful trip before the conference, no further airship construction would take place in the United Kingdom, so everything possible was done to get the airship finished in time. Yet it was not until the 1st of October that she was able to leave her shed again to undergo a week's further testing.

The great, cigar-shaped hulk slipped out of the shed and was tethered by the nose to its steel mooring tower. Built into the tower for the convenience of passengers was an electric lift. This, however, was not for the convenience of the crew who had to climb the 170 steps to get aboard.

Just after four o'clock that afternoon, the nose was detached from the moorings and the R.101 lifted into the air. The great silver airship with her engines throbbing cruised over London, Southend and the east coast before returning to Cardington the following morning. She had spent the night off Yarmouth before the flight back to base. The flight had been too short to prove her long-term reliability, and even on this twelve hour flight she had suffered engine trouble, though happily this had been rectified. In due course, the R.101 was granted her Certificate of Airworthiness, which was tantamount to giving the 'green light' for the trip to India. It was decided that she would depart on her maiden voyage to India on October 4th. All was prepared for the big day.

The commander of the R.101 for her first transcontinental flight was to be Flight Lieutenant H.C. Irwin. With him he would take forty-two officers and men, no less than five government dignitaries, including Lord Thomson, the Air Minister, complete with his personal valet, and six officials of the Royal Airship Works. This made a total list of fifty-four people.

On the appointed day they boarded the R.101 tethered to her mooring mast at Cardington. The air on board was one of excited expectancy as the crew went about the business of getting the ship ready for flight under the watchful eye of her commander. At 6.36 in the evening she cast off but as she did so, her nose dipped. Immediately Irwin jettisoned vast quantities of ballast water and in response the airship lifted away with her diesel engines roaring. On board, the passengers and crew watched the tower recede as she pulled up into the growing darkness.

Irwin nosed the airship around Bedford then set course for the south east. At last the R.101 was on her way but as she gained height it began to rain with growing intensity until a violent downpour soaked the silver skin of the airship. She crept on through the night at a snail's pace of 25 miles an hour flying at 1500 feet. The crew was disappointed with her performance, but it was a disappointment not shared by the passengers who were by then reclining in their luxurious surroundings enjoying the Champagne with which they were liberally plied. Some of those with a more technical turn of mind wandered round the vast airship examining its long galleries.

In the control cabin, Irwin tried not to show *his* disappointment at the ship's poor performance. He knew that he dared not venture higher for if he did the hydrogen gas inside the huge bags would expand as the air pressure outside lessened, running the risk of bursting the bags if the automatic release valves failed to operate. He had to content himself with flying on at that inadequate height. Not only did he have a height problem, the weather was beginning to turn sour and a forecast radioed to the R.101 from Cardington warned him of high-speed winds lying in his path.

Almost two hours after take off, the anxiously waiting people at Cardington received a wireless message from the R.101. It read:

'Over London. All well. Course now set for Paris. Intend to proceed via Paris, Tours, Toulouse and Narbonne.' In spite of the cheering message, however, all was not going well. The airship was reacting violently to the rain and the strong wind. She was rolling and pitching as she had never done before and this gave Irwin cause for concern.

As the airship slid over Hastings, Irwin received reports of violent storms over Southern France, an area he would have to fly over if he were to keep to his intended course. This message was quickly followed by an engine failure in one of the rear gondolas. It took some three hours to get the engine working properly again before the R.101 made off across the English Channel en route for France. By then they were flying so low that, even in the darkness, those on board could see the white-topped waves of the Channel below.

The great airship slipped over the coast of France and at

midnight, Cardington received another radio message.
'15 miles south of Abbeville. Average speed 30 knots.
Altimeter height 1500 feet. Weather intermittent rain....All
essential services now functioning satisfactorily.'

Just before 2 a.m., two French radio stations broadcast the
R.101's position to her and she duly acknowledged. That
acknowledgement was the last anyone was to hear from her.
Shortly after, the controller at Le Bourget airport in Paris
asked the R.101 for its flying speed. There was no reply. The
message was repeated but still there was silence. It soon
became evident that disaster had struck Britain's mightiest
airship.

Around 2 a.m. a French poacher, Eugene Rabouille, was
setting about his clandestine activities when his attention was
caught by the sound of engines. He stopped his work and his
eyes scanned the inky black sky for a sight of what he
thought must be an aeroplane. Then he saw the lights of the
airship flying very low. The noise of the engines grew in
intensity as the airship soared through the sky towards him
He stood riveted to the spot as the ship seemed to fill the air.
She was almost on the ground and obviously out of control.
Suddenly came the thunder of her hitting the ground as she
ploughed into a forest nearby. A fraction of a second later
what had been a dim silvery shape was transformed into a
welter of flame as 5½ million cubic feet of hydrogen ignited.
Rabouille heard a number of ear-splitting explosions and the
blast threw him to the ground where he lay horror struck, his
eyes glued to the wreckage of the great ship from which
tongues of flame were leaping hundreds of feet into the air.

In just a few seconds all that was left of the giant airship
was a grotesquely twisted frame of metal. All else had been
burned to a cinder by the intense heat. In the horror of that
disaster forty-eight people had perished but by some miracle,
six of the fifty-four people who had left Cardington survived.
They told later of the horror they had experienced....

Mr Leach, the foreman engineer of the R.101, told how at
2 a.m. he had just come off duty, having carried out a
detailed check of the engines. As he sat in the smoking room
relaxing after his tour of duty, he noticed that a soda syphon
and some glasses began to slide across the table. He deftly
caught them and replaced them.

'Must have dived a bit,' he thought. But then something

more disturbing happened. The telegraph warning bells began to jingle. Then the door of the smoking room crashed open and there in the corridor was a vast wall of flame. Only seconds later, the R.101 crashed.

The news of the crash numbed the British public. Like the *Titanic* disaster years earlier, this great queen of the air had perished on her maiden voyage. A court of enquiry was held which decided that the airship had stalled and plunged into the ground before anything could be done to get her out of the fatal stall. There were others, however, who had different ideas of what caused the crash. Some said that she broke her back in the air due to structural weakness. Others believed that the control cables had become jammed, forcing the airship down into the ground. Yet more experts put forward the theory that due to an alteration in barometric pressure the crew had misread the altimeter and imagined she was higher than in fact she was. It is extremely unlikely that anyone will ever know the real truth, for those who could tell the real truth perished in the crash.

What is absolutely certain is that, following the crash, airship production in Britain came to a halt, and was not even to be considered again for many years.

7
Alcock and Brown

Among the many 'famous firsts' of aviation history, the epic non-stop trans-Atlantic flight made by John Alcock and Arthur Whitten-Brown in June 1919 must rank as one of the greatest – not simply because it was a major stepping stone towards the jet airline services of today but because it was fraught with such terrible hazards. It was a stirring adventure in every possible way and one of the most dramatic flights ever made.

Even as early as the years immediately preceding the First World War there were men who had the vision to foresee a day when aircraft would be capable of flying all the way across the vast expanses of ocean and sea, which cover almost two thirds of the earth's surface. One such man was Lord Northcliffe, the British newspaper magnate who owned the *Daily Mail*. To induce men to turn their thoughts in the direction of long distance air travel he offered enormous prizes to airmen who could set up new records. Not long before war came he made an offer that was to have a profound effect upon aviation history. In the *Daily Mail* he said:-

'We offer £10,000 to the first person who crosses the Atlantic from any point in the United States, Canada or Newfoundland to any point in Great Britain or Ireland within 72 continuous hours. The flight may be made, of course, either way across the Atlantic. The prize is open to pilots of any nationality and machines of foreign as well as British construction.'

The offer took the flying world by storm. Ten thousand pounds was a vast sum of money in those days and a powerful incentive for aircraft designers and builders to think seriously about the possibility of trans-Atlantic flight. There was of course, one major drawback. As we have seen, the aircraft of that time were completely incapable of such a venture. The majority of them were light, single-engined planes capable of flying only short distances and even with drastic modifications could not undertake such a journey. The days of the multi-engined aircraft were near at hand but they had not yet come.

In spite of the fact that the aircraft were patently incapable of the job there were those who seriously began planning the attempt. But then war came and the offer had to be suspended for the duration of hostilities. It was, however, pretty obvious that it would be restarted after the end of the war. The challenge was by no means dead and many fliers continued to dream of the day when they would fly across the Atlantic. There were two in particular who spent many of the war years thinking of such a venture. They were John Alcock and Arthur Whitten-Brown who, quite by chance, were to meet after the war and take part in the great adventure. Two more contrasting characters it would have been difficult to meet.

Arthur Brown was born in Glasgow, the only son of American parents who eventually moved south to Manchester, where Arthur spent most of his childhood. As a child he was not a great fun-lover but rather a quiet, serious-minded boy. When he grew older, his sole interest was in engineering and he determined to carve out a career for himself in that highly-competitive industry. After a conventional schooling he went to serve his apprenticeship as an engineer and, with that completed, he was taken on by the

Westinghouse Company where he showed such promise that he was sent by them to South Africa. He returned to Britain just before the outbreak of war and enlisted in the army.

Eventually, Brown, intrigued by the new-fangled flying machines of the Royal Flying Corps, transferred to the air force, qualified as an observer and saw action in France. Then one day early in 1916, he and his pilot were on a routine patrol in their aircraft when they were attacked by German fighters and badly shot up by machine-gun fire. The aircraft was severely crippled by the attack and forced to land in enemy territory. During the crash landing, one of Brown's legs was badly injured and he suffered a wound that was to cripple him for the rest of his life and leave him in constant pain. Both he and his pilot were taken prisoner and after medical treatment, Brown was sent to a permanent prisoner-of-war camp. But the months that Brown spent in the p.o.w. camp were by no means wasted. Indeed, had it not been for his capture, he might never have become the famous aviator he did.

During these long months as a prisoner, Brown's thoughts were caught up in the intricacies of navigation and to occupy his mind he studied the subject in depth, particularly in relation to long distance flights over sea. He tried to apply the navigational techniques used by sailors to those which could be used by airmen. Becoming completely absorbed in the subject, he pondered on the possibilities of trans-Atlantic flight, remembering the *Daily Mail* prize.

For almost fourteen months, Brown remained a prisoner in Germany until, because of the severity of his leg wound, he was repatriated to Britain. He was regarded by the Germans as having been too badly disabled to fly again! Back in England he was posted to the Ministry of Munitions, working on the design of aircraft engines, but when the war ended he was demobilised and found himself out of a job. He was not to know it then, but unemployment was to bring a twist of fate, destined to make him world famous.

John Alcock was in almost every way different from Arthur Brown. He had an almost fanatical interest in engines and engineering. Alcock was born in Manchester in 1892 and from early childhood was fascinated by everything mechanical. He spent many a happy hour with his school friends tinkering with engines. As the aeroplane developed into a practical reality young John Alcock became more and more interested in it and in fact began to spend much of his spare time building model aircraft and real, working balloons. On more than one occasion, his efforts to build balloons were thwarted when the gas he used burst into flames and burnt his patiently-constructed balloons to cinders. But he remained undaunted and set about building others.

Alcock left school at the age of sixteen and became an apprentice mechanical engineer and it was during this apprenticeship that he first saw an air race. The race had been organised by the *Daily Mail* and took place over a course between London and Manchester. Eager as ever to catch sight of the competitors, John was at the airfield when the winner landed to the cheers of the waiting crowd. Watching the successful flier land, Alcock determined that he, too, would one day be a pilot.

There were, however, problems to becoming a pilot in those days. It cost quite a lot of money to train and young Alcock did not have the required amount. However, two years later, providence took a hand, one that was to change the whole course of John Alcock's life.

The company for which John worked was sent a damaged aeroplane engine for repair and when he saw it, young Alcock leapt at the chance of doing the repair work himself. He launched into it with vigour and made such a good job of it that he was allowed to take the engine back to the works at Brooklands, Weybridge, himself.

Brooklands was in those days the hub of British aviation where the major developments in the industry were made. It was naturally quite something for the flying-mad Alcock to visit this, the mecca of British aviation. It was while he was there that he discovered the engine belonged to no less a person than the great French pilot, Maurice Ducrocq. On seeing the excellent job Alcock had done on the engine and sensing the youngster's enthusiasm for flying, Ducrocq offered him a job as his personal mechanic. Alcock leapt at the chance.

From then on, there was no holding John Alcock back. He took every opportunity of working on all types of aircraft and grabbed every chance there was to get into the air. All the time he longed to become a pilot himself and it was Ducrocq who began giving him lessons. Alcock took to the air like a duck to water and after only two hours of flying instruction he flew solo, but he had to wait until he was twenty before he could finally qualify as a pilot and get the Royal Aero Club's Pilot's Certificate.

Now that he was a qualified pilot, Alcock indulged in all sorts of flying activities giving flying displays and testing new aircraft. It was not long before he was a pilot highly respected even by other more experienced fliers at Brooklands. But then in 1914 came the war. Alcock's reaction was immediate and he enlisted in the Royal Naval Air Service. Much to his annoyance, however, he was posted to a training squadron. Because of the demand for new pilots, his knowledge and flying experience were required in training. As all aircraft were required by the military, Alcock's newly-acquired Farman had to go with him. Training others to fly was tame stuff to a man of action like Alcock and he spent much of his time pestering the life out of the Admiralty to transfer him to an operational squadron. After months of waiting, his request was finally granted and he was posted to a base at Mudros in the Aegean Sea.

At that time, the Turks had sided with the Germans and it was to be against them that Alcock was to fight. His role was to be two-fold, that of fighter pilot and bomber pilot, since the machines he flew were capable of both these roles. It was not long after his arrival at Mudros that he chalked up his first 'kill' in the air and eventually his score rose to seven. Much of his time was taken up with bombing raids on Turkish military positions and shipping and in the summer of 1917 a new twin-engined Handley Page bomber was delivered to his squadron. This was what he had been waiting for because it had a considerable range and was capable of carrying, by the standards of those days, quite a considerable bomb-load.

Flying the bomber gave Alcock a great deal of experience of long distance flight under difficult conditions, something which was to prove invaluable to him in later years. Then on September 30th, 1917, he was at his base when a German photo-reconnaissance plane swept over Mudros, escorted by two fighters. Alcock saw it and leapt into action. He scrambled into a waiting fighter and zoomed into the sky where he shot down both the fighters then landed to the applause of his fellow pilots. Later that day, however, his luck was to change.

In the afternoon he was ordered off on a mission in a Handley Page bomber and took off with a full bomb load. As the aircraft neared its target, it came under heavy anti-aircraft fire and the port propeller was shattered. Using all his skill, Alcock managed to keep the aircraft stable but she was crippled so badly that he had to make a crash landing in the sea. He and his two man crew struggled onto the aircraft's wings as it floated but they immediately came under fire from snipers on the shore. They had no alternative but to swim for it and not long after reaching the beach they were picked up by the Turks and shepherded off to a p.o.w. camp.

The greatest ordeal for any prisoner is undoubtedly boredom and Alcock sought out some means of whiling away the days by finding an interest. Like Whitten-Brown his thoughts turned to the prospect of trans-Atlantic flight. He had behind him considerable experience of long-range flying and he set about the business of planning how he would set about such a flight. Sheer coincidence played a large part in the ultimate partnership of Alcock and Brown. Both had spent time in a prisoner-of-war camp and both had first had the idea of trans-Atlantic flight whilst prisoners.

It was not until the war was over and Alcock had returned to Brooklands to join the Vickers Company that their paths were destined to cross. The Vickers Company had built the highly successful Vickers Vimy bomber which they intended entering in the *Daily Mail* trans-Atlantic race. But others were just as anxious to beat them to the post. Certain major companies, not only in Britain but also in the United States, were hard at work, some constructing special aircraft for the bid while some like Vickers were converting their existing long-range aircraft. Alcock was the obvious choice for the job of piloting the aircraft but there was another problem, finding a navigator.

As luck would have it, Arthur Whitten-Brown was unemployed and scouting around the country trying desperately to find a job. Eventually his search brought him to Brooklands where he badgered the Vickers management into giving him an interview. He was lucky to get one since there were literally hundreds of ex-pilots and observers in exactly the same position as he was. But he had chosen the right moment to arrive.

Brown, on the surface, had no greater qualifications than many others who had been interviewed but when he told them of his studies of long-distance flight and oversea navigation in the prison camp, they offered him the job on the spot. He was just what they had been looking for. Brown was immediately introduced to Alcock who was at the time busy working on the plane. They took to each other right away and immediately got down to planning their trans-Atlantic trip. They knew they had competition from the other companies and also from the United States Navy which was planning to use flying boats to make the journey, although *their* intention was to do it in two hops, stopping off at the Azores en route. This of course barred them from getting the prize, but nevertheless they could be first across the Atlantic which would give them quite considerable national prestige. Time was of the essence for Alcock and Brown and the other companies were working all out to beat Vickers in the bid.

Three other British aircraft companies had entered for the race. The Martinsyde Company entered a single-engined biplane which was to be flown by Freddie Raynham with Captain Morgan as his co-pilot. Also the Sopwith Company was at work specially constructing another single-engined biplane to be piloted by Harry Hawker with Lieutenant Commander Mackenzie-Grieve as his navigator. Finally the Handley Page Company was going in for the race in a big way by entering a huge four-engined bomber to be flown by Major Brackley, who had been one of Alcock's pupils during his instructing days at the beginning of the war.

With each of the four companies working flat-out to finish their aeroplane before the others', time was fast running out, but both Alcock and Brown were determined that their Vimy should be as near perfect for the flight as possible and they spent many days making alterations to it to accommodate extra fuel and lessen weight. The biggest alteration of all was to the Vimy's bomb-bay which was replaced by a huge fuel tank. In spite of an all-out effort by the Vickers workers, it seemed that they were destined to be beaten by the others. Already two of the companies had shipped their aircraft out to Canada, and the other was almost complete and ready to go.

The decision to fly west to east across the Atlantic from

Canada was taken because the prevailing westerly winds in the Atlantic would give the aircraft the advantage of extra speed with the resulting saving in the weight of fuel to be carried. But to fly from the west meant dismantling the aeroplanes and sending them across the Atlantic in packing cases by boat to be rebuilt in Canada.

At last all was ready. Brown had collected the instruments he was to need for navigation and the finishing touches had been made to the Vimy. Flying tests had also been made by Alcock over long distances just to prove the durability of the Vimy. Everything had gone to their complete satisfaction.

After all the flying tests had been completed, the Vimy was taken apart and packed in special crates then loaded on board a freighter bound for Canada. With that done, Alcock and Brown boarded the ocean liner *Mauretania* and set sail. During the journey, Brown wasted not a minute. He spent a great deal of his time with the captain on the bridge, testing his theories of navigation at sea.

When they eventually arrived in Newfoundland they found to their dismay that the American flying boats were already there and waiting for the right weather to make the trip. The Vimy had not arrived by then and the first task facing the two aviators was to find an airfield from which they could take off on their trans-Atlantic bid. They had both thought that this could be done quite easily but they were shocked to find that all the open spaces, which had not already been reserved for the use of other aircraft, were cultivated and the farmers flatly refused to allow them to use them. The problem appeared insoluble and it seemed they were going to be beaten simply by the lack of a stretch of grass from which to take off. Disappointed but determined, they continued their search for a suitable field while the other pilots got ready. There was only one thing in their favour – the weather. It was atrocious, and if it held like that at least it would allow them time to find a field before the Vimy arrived from England.

It seemed, however, that their luck was out. They heard only four days after their arrival that three American flying boats had set off from Newfoundland in their bid to cross the Atlantic. They, it seemed, would beat them to it. As it turned out, one of the flying boats did make it across the Atlantic, becoming the first-ever aircraft to do so but it had done the journey in hops and therefore could not receive the prize. The greatest feat of all had yet to be achieved, that of flying non-stop across the ocean.

Although disappointed that they were not to be the first, Alcock and Brown carried on searching for a field. Then one day they returned to their hotel to find that both Hawker and Raynham had left. Hawker was by then well on his way but disaster had struck Raynham, who had crashed on take off. Fortunately neither he nor his navigator had been seriously hurt. But the fact that Hawker had gone stunned Alcock and Brown. They need not, however, have worried for, as it turned out, Hawker was destined to crashland in the sea only five hundred miles from his goal. Luckily for Hawker he landed the aircraft near to a steamer and was picked up and taken to Scotland. The steamer was not equipped with radio and it was five days before Alcock and Brown finally discovered what had become of Hawker.

On the 26th of May Alcock and Brown watched the freighter carrying the Vimy dock and the bomber was duly unloaded. Their luck was in for the following day they were offered a field from which to take off. It was known as Lester's Field, a rough stretch of grassland where horses were put out to graze. This they decided would have to do and they set about the business of transforming it from an uneven, moundy piece of ground into a workable runway. Trees had to be felled and great mounds flattened.

As the days passed the team of mechanics which had come over specially from England made good progress on re-building the Vimy, but then they struck a major problem The fuel which had been brought over from England for the flight was found to be useless and it was not until the 12th of June that another supply arrived.

At last they were able to make a test flight during which part of the undercarriage fell off, so the big day had to be postponed again. It was not until the 14th of June that everything was ready for the flight. The weather was good and the Vimy was in tip-top working order. Then as the mechanics were manhandling the aircraft to the take-off point, one of the fuel pipes became fractured. With all speed that was fixed. Finally, after all their trials and tribulations. Alcock and Brown were ready to go. The most dramatic flight of the century was about to begin.

Both men put on their specially heated flying suits and climbed aboard. They sat closely together in the cramped, open cockpit, and Alcock began the final checks before take-off. Then with these done, the two engines burst into life, one after the other, while Brown made a last-minute check on his instruments. The engines roared as Alcock ran them up and it took forty stout men to hold the aircraft back. Then he throttled down while the men got out of the way.

The Vimy rocked and vibrated as the engines were run up to full power and the bomber eased forward and gathered speed. She wobbled along the runway for some three hundred yards before finally lifting into the air. They were off.

Alcock swung the huge bomber inland to gain height then roared across the field in a final farewell before setting course out to sea. Between them and Ireland lay 1890 miles of violent sea and a multitude of hazards many of which they could not possibly have foreseen.

At almost 4.30 that afternoon they crossed the coast of Newfoundland and Brown radioed back to base that they had reached the sea. The weather was good then and while these favourable conditions prevailed, Brown went about the business of 'shooting' the stars with his sextant.

For half an hour they flew on through the clear, bright sky then ahead of them they saw their first obstacle, a gigantic bank of thick fog which completely obscured the horizon. They had no alternative but to fly straight into it. As the aircraft plunged into the fog, visibility was cut to only a couple of yards and the wet vapour swirled into the open cockpit, soaking the two men inside.

Brown, desperate to keep right on track, could not take sightings in the fog so he motioned to Alcock to climb and the aircraft struggled higher. Soon they emerged from the bank of sea fog only to find themselves in clear air between the fog and dense cloud above. Brown had no alternative but to navigate by dead reckoning.

The noise from the two engines was deafening and neither man could be heard by the other. In order to communicate they had to write each other notes and pass them over, a system made doubly difficult by the moisture in the cockpit which soaked the paper on which they wrote.

Having determined his exact position, Brown set about tapping out a message to their base on his morse key but no sooner had he started than the transmitter went completely dead. Something was wrong and he found out exactly what it was when he glanced out at the struts which stretched between the biplane's wings. The little generator off which the transmitter worked had lost its wind propeller. Now the wireless was out of action, they were absolutely cut off from the rest of the world with no means of communication should they get into difficulties. A feeling of complete isolation crept over the two aviators but they flew on, gradually gaining height as they progressed. However, more trouble was not far off. Suddenly there was a loud *crack* from the starboard engine. Almost at once flames began belching out of the exhaust and the engine roared in a deafening crescendo of sound. But by some miracle it still continued to run remarkably smoothly.

They had been in the air for only two hours and already they had suffered two major setbacks; a useless wireless and an engine that might stop at any moment. They had no alternative but to press on. It was then just a little after six o'clock in the evening and they decided to eat some food. This they did then they settled down to work again with Alcock nursing the Vimy through the foul weather.

Their position in the cockpit could not have been less comfortable. Soaking moisture seemed to get every-where....into their clothes, making them shiver continually with cold and misting up Alcock's goggles so that he could barely see. He became so infuriated with this that he finally threw the goggles into the ocean and flew on with unguarded eyes.

It was not until after eight o'clock that evening that a break in the clouds finally came and Brown was able to check their position. To his surprise and delight he found that they were only slightly off course. A correction was made but no sooner had Alcock swung the aircraft round onto the correct bearing than the patch of sky disappeared and they were enshrouded in thick, wet cloud once more, feeling their way blindly onwards.

In spite of the faulty engine, Alcock succeeded in coaxing the Vimy higher into the sky through the murk and the growing darkness but then more trouble overtook them. The heating system in their specially-made flying suits failed and they were chilled to the bone. Freezing and shivering with the icy cold they flew until, at last, just after midnight, the Vimy broke through the cloud and they emerged in a star-lit heaven. With the moon shining brightly down on them they flew on over the seemingly never-ending expanse of cloud.

All the time that they cruised on, Brown's leg was agonisingly painful. The cramped conditions in the cockpit did not allow him to exercise it at all and the result was continuous pain but not once did he complain to Alcock. He bravely kept quiet and allowed Alcock to concentrate all his efforts on flying the aircraft.

The long-distance flier's greatest enemy was beginning to attack them....tiredness. Both men had to fight against sleep all the way and the result of this tiredness produced weird effects, particularly upon Brown, who began to have strange visions. The clouds took on the appearance of grotesque monsters illuminated by the moonlight. Brown realising what was happening, did all he could to fight against it, but the visions kept recurring until finally the first light of dawn appeared over the horizon. Just as it did so, however, they were suddenly immersed in a great wall of cumulo-nimbus cloud. It was like being cast into a black cauldron of boiling air. In an instant, the Vimy was completely out of control, tossed about the sky by the violent draughts of air. Lightning flashed, momentarily casting a diffused light over the plane which was by then tumbling towards the sea with the deafening roar of thunder torturing their ear drums. They had become completely disorientated. Without a horizon by which to determine whether or not he was flying straight and level, Alcock had no idea in which direction they were heading. A glance at the altimeter gave him the horrible truth in an instant....

Alcock fought with the controls in a bid to get the Vimy out of its dive but at first he fought in vain. Then pulling back on the throttle he at last managed to take the power off the two engines before they were irreparably damaged by racing out of control. Using sheer brute force, Alcock hauled back on the control column and mercifully the Vimy levelled out....only one hundred feet above the swirling Atlantic waves. They were so close to the waves that they could feel the spray from them on their faces.

When they had regained their composure after their close shave, Brown glanced at his compass only to discover that they were heading directly back towards Newfoundland. When Brown pointed this out to Alcock they both burst out in peals of laughter. The tension of the situation was suddenly broken and Alcock wheeled the aircraft round onto the proper course.

It took almost an hour to get back to their original cruising height but again they found themselves flying in terrible weather with heavy, driving rain pouring into the cockpit and leaving their feet in growing puddles of water. Then came hail, biting and cutting into their faces. As a final addition to their troubles, it began to snow.

The snow and cold began to ice up the engines as they inched higher into the sky and the possibility of the engines failing soon turned to a terrifying probability. Somehow they had to be cleared of ice and this could only be done by one of them going out on to the wings to chip away the steadily growing accumulation. Since Alcock had to fly the aircraft, the job fell to Brown. In spite of his injured and aching leg he clambered out of the cockpit and onto the wing, clinging to the struts for dear life lest he be swept off and into the sea. He edged his way along until he reached the engine, while Alcock did all in his power to keep the aircraft straight and level, a difficult enough job with so much turbulence. In all, Brown went out onto the wings *six* times. For a crippled man this was a truly staggering feat of courage.

Meanwhile Alcock nursed the Vimy higher in a bid to get free of the cloud and lift the aircraft into the sun, but as they climbed the ice was getting thicker on the control surfaces of the Vimy and Alcock had to use all his strength to keep the aircraft flying. At last as they reached 11,000 feet, they broke through into the sun and Brown quickly took a bearing. They were bang on course for Ireland. But no sooner had Brown passed on the good news than the starboard engine began to cough and splutter. It was completely blocked up by snow and looked as if it might stop any moment. There was only one thing for it....get down as low as possible. Alcock cut both engines and pushed forward the control column putting the Vimy into a shallow dive through the dense cloud. At last they levelled off at 1000 feet and the ice began to melt away from the engines and control surfaces.

They descended even further and finally settled down at 500 feet. Alcock restarted the engines and breathed a sigh of relief when they burst into life and worked perfectly.

On they flew, munching sandwiches to keep up their strength and straining their eyes for a sight of land which they thought must be somewhere ahead of them Then suddenly it was there – a cluster of small islands which Brown quickly reckoned were part of a group off the coast of Connemara. They were overcome with joy when they at last swept over the tiny dots then on over the coast.

As they cruised over the green pastures below, Alcock scanned the landscape, looking for a place to put down and finally decided on what looked like a flat stretch of grass. He swung the aircraft round in a tight turn and began his approach run..Down they went. They got closer and closer to the patch of green as the aircraft lost height. Alcock cut his engines for the landing. It was then that he realised his terrible mistake. The patch of green was not firm turf but a marshy bog. It was too late to do anything then and they touched down, remaining upright for a short distance before the wheels dug into the bog and the plane came to a sudden halt, tipping up on its nose. For a moment all was silent, then the two men, miraculously unhurt, clambered out of the cockpit and dropped onto the marshy ground. They had made it!

Deafened after the continuous roar of the engines in their ears for so long, neither of them could make out what the other was saying so they gave up and just stood there, marvelling at their success. They were soon surrounded by an excited crowd of Irishmen who at first could not believe that the two men had flown across the Atlantic until one of them produced a bag of mail which they had carried with them.

Within hours, the news of their arrival was being flashed across the world. They were heroes, the first men ever to fly non-stop across the Atlantic Ocean. The flight had taken them 15 hours and 57 minutes from coast to coast. It brought them both fame and fortune as well as knighthoods for their services to aviation, an accolade which both of them richly deserved. Alas, Alcock was not to live to enjoy the fruits of his achievement. He was killed only a few months later during a flight in bad weather. Sir Arthur Whitten-Brown, the survivor of that famous duo, was horror-struck at the loss of his friend and gave up flying to return to engineering.

Alcock and Brown, more than any others, proved beyond doubt that trans-Atlantic flight was here to stay. They turned a pipe dream into a reality and paved the way for the Jumbo jets and supersonic Concordes of today.

8

The Spirit of St. Louis

In the early morning of the 20th May, 1927, a young American pilot climbed into the cramped cockpit of a Ryan Monoplane and took off from Roosevelt Field, on the outskirts of New York to attempt the first *solo* crossing of the Atlantic Ocean. The flight this man was about to undertake was destined to become the most publicised in the annals of aviation history. He was Charles Augustus Lindbergh, the man who was to succeed where others had tragically failed.

Lindbergh was born in Detroit, Michigan, on the 4th February, 1902, the son of a famous American lawyer of Swedish descent. The Lindbergh family had been among the early American pioneers who had had to survive the rigours of the early settlement days, scratching a living from the land and fighting off hostile Indians to protect their claims. It was because of this family background and influence that Lindbergh grew to be tenacious and determined in everything he did.

Lindbergh's father, who was later to become a famous congressman, was the greatest influence upon Charles' life. He believed in his boy being self-reliant and completely capable of looking after himself. Self-confidence, honesty and determination were the qualities essential to a happy and successful life, Lindbergh senior believed, and he brought up his son with this in mind, giving Charles every opportunity of proving himself, no matter what the situation or the consequences.

From a very early age, Charles, like so many other great aviators, had shown a strong interest in machines. He marvelled at the motor car and its intricate workings and took delight in pottering about with engines, trying to find out why and how they 'ticked'. His father, always anxious to develop any interest Charles might have, presented him with a car when he was still young and in fact not quite big enough to drive it.He believed in throwing Charles in at the deep end so to speak and right from the very start Charles was allowed to drive the car by himself. This, however, produced its quota of hair-raising moments. Once, when out driving with his father, he was motoring down a hill towards a railway crossing. As the car neared the crossing he applied the brake....but nothing happened. To make matters worse, there was a fast freight train hurtling towards the crossing. He knew he must act quickly or they would collide. His father, determined to see how Charles would react to get them out of the situation, sat motionless beside his son, refusing to come to his aid. Charles knew his father only too well and realised that he was entirely on his own. Just then he spotted a ditch near the railway track. That, he thought, was the only way out. With the car steadily gathering speed, he swerved into the ditch. There was an almighty crash as they plunged into it and came to an abrupt halt just as the train was thundering by. Bruised, but still alive, father and son scrambled out of the car. Charles had done exactly what his father would have done and he earned his father's respect because of it.

Young Lindbergh's interest in machines and engineering grew as he got older and at school he showed little interest in anything else. He developed into a modest, almost retiring young man absorbed in his subject, until one day in Washington he caught sight of an aeroplane. He marvelled at the effortless-seeming way in which it soared through the air, and he determined that one day he would have a crack at flying. After all, aircraft had engines and these were his first love.

In due course, Charles enrolled at the University of Wisconsin where he studied chemical engineering, but the thought of that aeroplane and the excitement of flight kept prodding him as he carried on with his studies. He could not get aviation out of his mind and finally after the end of his third term, he left university and began pilot training with the Nebraska Aircraft Corporation. That was on All Fools Day, April 1st, 1922, three years after Alcock and Brown had made their epic Atlantic crossing in the Vickers Vimy. The day after joining the company, Charles Lindbergh made his first flight in an aeroplane and from then on the urge to fly was never to leave him. Lindbergh revelled in every minute he was in the air, drinking in the thrill of flight and eagerly waiting for the next time. The opportunities for flying were many that spring for Charles was the only pupil at the school.

In those early days of aviation, the pilot was expected to be proficient not only in flying the plane but also in maintaining it. He had to know everything there was to know about it and be able to service the aeroplane and replace spare parts. So whenever he was not flying, Lindbergh was clad in overalls and tinkering with the engines.

Only two months after beginning flying training, Charles' instructor thought he was ready to make his first solo flight, but there was a problem. It was one of the company's rules that a substantial deposit had to be put down by the pupil against the possibility of him crashing or destroying the aircraft on his first solo....and Charles just could not raise the money to pay. He had to postpone working for the company but in the meantime he was determined to get in as much flying as he possibly could, so he went 'barn-storming.'

Barn-storming was a popular job for pilots in the United States during the 1920s. These dare-devil young aviators equipped with obsolete World War One aircraft toured the States, giving hair-raising exhibitions of stunt flying in towns and villages. Lindbergh joined one of these 'circuses' and performed such feats of daring that he was soon billed as 'Daredevil Lindbergh'. His courage in the air was almost unbelievable and he soon became a star of the show, doing crazy things like hand-stands on the aircraft's wings while it zoomed past the awe-struck spectators. He even went in for parachuting and perfected the technique of the 'double drop'. He would leap out of an aeroplane and pull the rip-cord of his parachute then cut the cords and tumble headlong towards the ground before opening a second 'chute. This soon became the highlight of the show and fully justified his title of 'Daredevil'.

As his success as a barn-stormer grew, he earned more and more money which he quickly deposited in the bank, determined as ever to fly solo. After several months he was not only able to fly solo for the first time but to buy his own aircraft, a Curtiss 'Jenny' for which he paid five hundred dollars.

Without wasting time, he put the aircraft to work and continued flying around America offering townsfolk rides in his aircraft at five dollars a time. To Lindbergh, even the months when he was almost broke, were enjoyable. He was flying and that was the most important thing in his life. It was not, however, all fun. Because he could not afford to employ an assistant he had to do all his own repairs and maintenance to the Curtiss. Luckily he had been expertly trained for just that.

The Curtiss Jenny was, by the standards of the day, not much of an aeroplane. It did not have the powerful engines that the U.S. Army Air Service aircraft had and Lindbergh longed to fly these. He thought things over and decided that the only way to widen his scope and experience as a pilot was to join the Army Air Service. This he did but to his surprise he had to go right through pilot training once more. The army would not accept his pilot's certificate, so for the fifteen months that followed he went through the procedure again, but this time on much more sophisticated and faster aircraft types.

Lindbergh's training was not without incident and one day he had good cause to be grateful for his skill as a parachutist. He was flying with his squadron and engaging in mock dog-fights when he crashed into another fighter in mid air. Both aircraft were extensively damaged and plummeted towards the ground with Lindbergh and the other pilot fighting their way out of their cockpits. Luckily both of them landed safely without as much as a scratch.

Having gained all the experience he could in flying military aircraft, Lindbergh left the U.S. Army Air Service and looked around for another job. As it turned out, he could not have left at a more opportune moment for at this time the U.S. Postal Service was thinking of opening up air mail services throughout the United States and was keen to engage young pilots for the job of carrying mail the length and breadth of the country. The prospect of such a job excited Lindbergh who had heard of the exploits of some of the pioneer airmen in this field.

Flying the mail was possibly one of the most hazardous flying jobs of all in those days. The postal companies were interested in only one thing — getting the mail through — and fast, no matter what the cost. They were not unduly concerned about trifles like storms, blizzards or thunder and lightning. The mail must get through and it was up to the pilot to see that it did....come what might. The job was not made easier by the types of aeroplanes the pilots were required to fly. They were generally antiquated First World War types which should long before have been out of service.

In spite of all the hazards built into such a job, Lindbergh saw it as a challenge and one he could not resist. He was duly appointed chief pilot in the Robertson Aircraft Corporation, which had won a contract to carry mail between the cities of St. Louis and Chicago. It was a small company, short of money and had some of the oldest aeroplanes imaginable.

Before he took off on his first mail-carrying flight he was briefed on his responsibilities. The most important thing in the aircraft was the mail. If he was obliged to crash land or bale out, his first duty was to retrieve the mail from the wreckage and get it on the next train for delivery!

The difficulties in flying these old aircraft were enormous, especially because their instruments were so primitive. They had no cockpit lighting for flying at night and navigation during the hours of darkness was carried out with the use of a survey map and a hand torch. To add to the misery of flying such machines, Lindbergh was often obliged to fly through the worst possible weather as a result of which he came to grief on more than one occasion and often had to parachute to safety. In spite of these mishaps, he achieved the best record of all the air mail companies with a 90% success rate, quite an accomplishment considering the conditions under which he had to fly, without radio or proper navigational aids such as beacons to guide him.

Much of the time in the air, flying these mail routes, was spent looking down at familiar ground and Lindbergh came to know the routes like the back of his hand. Indeed he knew them so well that he flew them almost automatically. It was while he was day-dreaming that he remembered the incident which had occurred in 1919 when Raymond Orteig, a New York hotel owner, had offered a prize of 25,000 dollars to the first man to fly solo across the Atlantic Ocean. Up till then no one had succeeded, although many had tried.

The thought of a flight across the Atlantic fired Lindbergh's imagination and on these lonely flights between St. Louis and Chicago he thought deeply about undertaking such a venture himself. He planned things in detail but of course the major problem was money. It would take considerable funds to finance such a venture.

Lindbergh was not the only one who was at that time planning a trans-Atlantic flight. There were others; many of them well-known, highly experienced pilots such as René Fonck, the World War One French fighter ace. This was 1926 and the race to be the first man across the Atlantic was at its height. If he were to stand any chance at all of making the bid and succeeding, he would have to act fast.

One day, however, he hit on an idea....one that might give him the money he would need. Lindbergh was banking for his money on the pride of the city fathers and businessmen of St. Louis, which had become his adopted home. He duly approached them and, using the best 'sales talk' he could muster, tried to point out how advantageous it would be to the prestige of the great city of St. Louis if its businessmen were seen by all the United States to be men of vision, keeping up with the new age of aviation, men who were willing to invest their money for its furtherance. If he were successful, Lindbergh pointed out, St. Louis would be put right on the map and the resulting publicity could do nothing but good for the city. The wise businessmen of St. Louis were very impressed with Lindbergh's scheme and agreed to back him to the tune of 16,000 dollars. This was quite a sizable sum in those days, and their readiness to produce it showed in no small measure their confidence in the young, comparatively unknown, pilot.

Lindbergh's first major problem was to find a suitable aeroplane and to do this he set off for California to visit the Ryan Airline Company. The instant enthusiasm for the project shown by all the members of the Ryan staff impressed Lindbergh and he and a design team got down to work. They laboured day and night and eventually the design for the Ryan Monoplane emerged. With Lindbergh watching over their shoulders, the team planned the monoplane incorporating every feature he wanted. Then came the business of actually building the machine. Time was running out and the men of the Ryan factory worked day and night, some of them not leaving their work benches for days on end, grabbing snatches of sleep only when they were too exhausted to work.

Such was Lindbergh's eye for detail and careful planning that he had taken everything into consideration when they designed the aircraft. Nothing had been left to chance.

The most important factor as far as Lindbergh was concerned was the aircraft's range. The distance between New York and Paris, the destination he would be aiming for, was some 3610 miles but he made sure that the design of the aircraft would allow it to fly at least 4000 miles. Not an inch of space was wasted. Every nook and cranny was designed to take fuel to give the Ryan a longer range. Weight, too, was a problem. The heavier the aircraft, the more fuel it would burn. So Lindbergh did without a parachute. No night-flying instruments would be included and many other instruments which most pilots thought vital for a crossing he discarded.

When it was eventually rolled out of the hanger, the Ryan Monoplane was christened the *'Spirit of St. Louis'* in honour of the city which had put up the money for it and had backed Lindbergh so fully.

Thé Ryan was powered by the most modern type of engine available at the time, a Wright Whirlwind radial. Construction of the aircraft had taken only sixty days, a remarkable feat of production and team co-ordination. Meanwhile, Lindbergh threw himself into the study of navigation. He was an expert in the art of navigation over land where there were generally masses of landmarks to point the way to a destination, but he had no knowledge of navigation over sea and this he saw as one of his major obstacles. He got down to work poring over books well into

the night until he was so expert on the subject that he even
gave a lecture on it to a group of naval cadets.

The day came, on the 28th of April, 1927, when the *Spirit
of St. Louis* was ready for her first flight. Lindbergh took her
into the air for the first time and she handled beautifully. Her
performance was well beyond the wildest dreams of her
designers and Lindbergh could not have been more pleased.
Further tests were carried out and minor modifications made
until he was one hundred per cent sure that the *Spirit of St.
Louis* could do the job.

Yet it seemed that Lindbergh might be pipped at the post
because news reached him that another aircraft had left
France to attempt the crossing. Then he heard, a few days
later, that the French plane was overdue. The aircraft had
crashed. Another brave aviator had fallen to the dangers of
the Atlantic. The death toll was mounting and this gave the
sceptics, who doubted the wisdom of Lindbergh's attempt,
more ammunition. Lindbergh was now even more determined
in his aim to succeed.

To prove to the sceptics that his plane was all he thought
it, Lindbergh decided to fly the Ryan from San Diego,
California, to St. Louis instead of sending it by road. This, he
thought, would show that the Ryan was capable of long
flights without trouble, even though the distance between
these two cities was only half that between New York and
Paris.

He set off over the Californian Mountains on the 10th May
on his way to St. Louis. All went well until he was over
Arizona when the engine began to play up, missing beats and
spluttering ominously. Would this be the end of Lindbergh's
dream? He tried to work out what was wrong and frantically
checked his instruments. All seemed in order but the engine
continued to play up. Then just as quickly as it had started
the trouble disappeared and the engine ran smoothly all the
way to St. Louis where he arrived to a hero's welcome.

Two days later he left St. Louis to rousing cheers and set
course for New York, the place from which he aimed to take
off on his trans-Atlantic flight. He was not prepared for the
reception committee that awaited him at Curtiss Field on the
outskirts of the city. Reporters and photographers from all
the leading newspapers were there waiting for him. Lindbergh
had not until then been exposed to the glare of publicity and

for the rather modest, retiring young man it came as something of a shock. He was hounded by the press everywhere he went and bombarded with questions about all sorts of irrelevant things. He soon came to the conclusion that it would be a blessed relief to be out over the Atlantic and on his own.

Lindbergh spent the next few days busy with technicians making the final checks before the flight. Every minute detail had to be double-checked to ensure success, but there was no shortage of willing hands to help him.

At last all was ready for the flight to begin but now the weather took a turn for the worse. Every day that passed meant the chance that some other aviator might beat him to the post. He prayed that there would be a break in the weather and on the morning of the 20th May, 1927, it came. The weather forecast was at last promising and at 7.30 that morning, the *Spirit of St. Louis* was completely fuelled up and ready to go. Lindbergh's epic adventure was about to begin.

With a cheery wave to his friends congregated around the aircraft, Lindbergh clambered into the cockpit and closed the door. Ahead of him lay a journey of 3610 miles over a watery waste and for provisions he took with him only a canteen of water and a brown paper bag with a few sandwiches. His one major obstacle on the journey would be staying awake and he reckoned that he had a better chance of doing that on an empty stomach.

The cockpit of the Ryan was so designed that Lindbergh could not see ahead. His vision was obscured by the huge radial engine and the main fuel tank. In order to see where he was going he had installed a periscope.

He carried out his pre-flight checks, then signalled to the ground crew to pull the chocks away. The Whirlwind engine roared at full throttle then the din died and he eased off the brakes. The *Spirit of St. Louis* rolled over the uneven grass perimeter track then swung into wind. This was to be the telling time. Heavily laden with fuel, the Ryan was at her maximum weight for take-off. Others who had attempted the Atlantic crossing had come to grief on take-off when their over-weighted aircraft had failed to lift off the ground and crashed at the end of the runway.

Lindbergh eased open the throttle and the Whirlwind

roared. Brakes off and she rolled along the runway, with Lindbergh's friends running alongside. yelling encouragement. The speed gathered and the runway sped past beneath the monoplane until the tail lifted into the air. The end of the runway was coming dangerously close and Lindbergh fought to get her off the ground. His eyes were glued to the speedometer. Gradually the needle crept up to the take-off speed. He pulled back on the control column, the *Spirit of St. Louis* lifted into the air only to bump again on the ground and bounce into the air once more. This time she stayed airborne and swept over the end of the runway clearing some telegraph wires by a mere twenty feet. Lindbergh was on his way.

The *Spirit of St. Louis* pulled away over Long Island as Lindbergh willed her higher and higher into the air until he reached his cruising height, then he settled down to the business of navigating the aircraft along the New England coast. The first couple of hours went well with a strong tail wind to help him on his way, then he flew over Cape Cod. Now he was over a vast expanse of sea. From this time on he would no longer be navigating by conventional means, he would be flying almost entirely over the sea. There lay ahead of him a flight of 250 miles before he reached Nova Scotia, so now he had to use his Mercator's projection of the Atlantic with the thin line of his course traced on it.

The Ryan flew on over the sea without problems but Lindbergh was already beginning to feel tired. The monotony of the journey was beginning to send him to sleep, so he swept down towards the rolling waves and flashed across them, darting at mast height through fishing fleets and waving to the crews who gaped open-mouthed as he raced by. But even this little diversion was not having the desired effect. His legs and back ached through inactivity and there was a terrible desire to allow his eyes to close into sleep. But he fought against the temptation. He had a long way ahead of him so he pulled open a side window in the cabin and the icy air swept in, bringing him back to life with a jolt.

It was not until after mid-day that Lindbergh first caught sight of the coast of Nova Scotia. He'd done it and, to his amazement, he was only six miles out in his navigation....not bad on a 250 mile trip. The first hurdle had been surmounted and he flew on to St. Johns where he swept over

Lester's Field, waving to the astonished people at the airfield who cheered him on his way. Lindbergh had deviated slightly from his original route with good cause. He knew that the staff at Lester's Field would wire New York telling his friends that they had spotted the *Spirit of St. Louis* and they would know that he had got at least that far safely. Furthermore if he did happen to come down in the Atlantic shortly after crossing the coast, the searchers would have a more positive idea of where he was.

Soon the land slipped away beneath the plane and the *Spirit of St. Louis* nosed out over the Atlantic. Lindbergh's greatest trial was just beginning. Ahead lay thousands of miles of trackless sea with almost every hazard a pilot could dream of.

The controls on the monoplane were designed to react to even the slightest touch. The gentlest nudge on the control column or the rudder pedals meant a change in course. Lindbergh had planned it that way, for he reasoned that if the controls were sluggish and the aircraft too stable there would be a tendency for him to let it do all the work and fall asleep. The result of that would be disastrous. So he had literally to *fly* the aircraft all the way, never allowing his concentration to lapse.

There was a long way to go before his first landfall, the coast of Ireland, but so far the plane had cruised through the sky without any trouble. All was going according to plan. He swept on over the water which was dotted with great icebergs jutting out of the rolling waves and punctuating the darkening sea as the sun fell behind the horizon. Soon he was plunged into an Atlantic darkness with only his few instruments to guide him over the sea.

As he progressed, it became bitterly cold and ahead of him he could see great mountainous pillars of thick, black storm clouds. His fuel capacity did not allow him the luxury of flying around the storm that lay in his path so he was forced to head right into the teeth of it. Sweeping into the cloud, the currents of air caught the Ryan and tossed her about the sky like a feather. Lindbergh had a real struggle with the controls to keep the plane stable.

The storm continued to rage as he ploughed his way through it, then the worst happened. Flashing his torch out through the window he could see ice forming on the wings.

This, if it got worse, could spell doom for him. 'Icing-up' greatly impaired the lift ability of the wings and also affected the operation of the ailerons and elevators as well as the rudder. If these were to become locked he would crash out of control.

To Lindbergh's relief, the weather grew steadily better as he progressed through the last part of the storm and the ice slowly disappeared from the wings. But his problems were far from over, there was another, equally deadly one overtaking him.

He, like other Atlantic fliers, began to see things and have visions. The clouds transformed themselves into all sorts of weird shapes like giant monsters in the sky, waiting to swallow up his aircraft. All this was the result of tiredness. How was he to fight off this terrible urge to sleep when even at that point he was barely half way to his destination?

He sipped at his water and continually kept himself busy by filling in his log book with meticulous care. He had been in the air for more than sixteen hours and he had almost reached the point of total exhaustion – but he drove himself on. He had no alternative. One careless slip would send him careering into the waves.

At last dawn came but even then he could not shake off the urge to sleep. He found himself plunging from one great mass of fog or cloud headlong into another. The swirling fog seemed endless. More mirages appeared before his eyes. He saw land which turned out to be nothing more than another low bank of fog and he even imagined he could see beaches with rolling hills behind them. All were figments of his imagination.

In a sort of half consciousness he flew on and it was not until he had been flying for almost twenty-seven hours that he caught sight of something in the water. 'Could it be another mirage?' he thought. He dipped the aircraft towards it and the dot soon took on the shape of a small boat – an *inshore* fishing boat! Unable to believe his eyes, he swept even lower and circled the boat.

It was definitely one of the small, inshore types. This meant only one thing.....he must be close to Ireland. Then there were more boats...a whole fleet of them. He flew alongside one of them, opened his window and actually shouted to the fisherman on board the boat.

'Which way to Ireland?' he yelled. But the fishermen were too astonished to reply and Lindbergh flew on. Peering through his periscope he kept a watchful eye on the horizon, searching for the slightest sign of land. Then, suddenly, it was there and at last he crossed the coast. Checking his map he discovered that it was in fact the south west coast of Ireland. He had made it that far and his success gave him new heart. But there was still a long way to go. He crossed the southernmost tip of Ireland and then the Irish Sea until he was cruising over the Cornish coast of England and could set course for France. Darkness closed in once more and it was night when he crossed the French coast.

Following the navigational beacons between the coast and Paris, he finally caught sight of the brightly-lit city at ten o'clock that evening. Searchlights swept the sky in greeting as Lindbergh nosed down towards Le Bourget airport. As he neared the ground he could see streams of cars pouring along the roads towards the airport. News of his arrival had travelled fast and it seemed that everyone in Paris wanted to be there when he touched down.

Minutes later, the *Spirit of St. Louis* slipped onto the runway at Le Bourget. The greatest flight of all time had been completed. Charles Lindbergh had fulfilled his life's ambition and had almost overnight become the most celebrated airman in aviation history.

9
The First Lady of Flying

By 1928 the Atlantic Ocean had been crossed by air no fewer than ten times, but even so it was still a dangerous undertaking. There were, however, men prepared to take the risk to list their names amongst the pioneers headed by Alcock and Brown. Two such men were Americans Lou Gordon and Wilmer Stultz who planned to make the crossing in that year.

It occurred to the two men and their friend and aviation enthusiast George Putnam Palmer, a New York publisher, that only *men* had so far flown the Atlantic. What a gimmick and boost for the prestige of American womanhood if they could take a woman along with them. The more they thought about it, the more enthusiastic they became. But there was a problem. Where would they get a young woman willing to risk possible death amid the Atlantic waves?

At once a nation-wide search began, led by Palmer who interviewed a host of willing candidates. Alas, none of them was really suitable. Above all they needed a stable, 'down to earth' woman with just the right degree of self-confidence and one who would not panic in an emergency. So far none of the girls Palmer had interviewed had all the necessary qualities. When he had almost exhausted his supply of candidates, he searched his mind for others, running through the list of lady friends he had. It was then that he remembered a young girl teacher and social worker he had known for some time. He decided to get in touch with her and see if she was interested.

Palmer's friend had, he remembered, flown with Frank Hawkes, one of America's famous barn-stormers who performed feats of daring in the air to excited crowds across America. Then, he recalled, she had herself become a pilot but lack of money had forced her to give it up. This girl, he thought, might just be the one he was looking for. Little did he know then that she was to become one of the most famous pilots ever to take to the air. Her name was Amelia Earhart.

So it was that the tall, thirty-year-old girl with the short, unkempt tawny hair walked eagerly into his office, trying desperately not to show too much enthusiasm and excitement. Amelia was attractive in a sort of boyish way with her short hair, her freckled face and open grey eyes. She certainly didn't look her thirty years.

Palmer and Amelia talked at some length about her experience of flying; what she had done, whom she had flown with and the most important question of all, whether or not she would like to fly the Atlantic with Gordon and Stultz. For Amelia the question need never have been asked. It was obvious to Palmer, a particularly good judge of character, that he had found his girl. She was just what he had been looking for. The answer was an emphatic 'yes'. Palmer pointed out the many hazards she was likely to face on such a trip but Amelia merely replied that she would not consider going on the trip if there was not an element of danger. She loved a challenge and regarded life as not worth living without one.

Soon everything was arranged and the long, tiring flight with all its dangers took place. Throughout the flight, the inexhaustible Amelia spent most of her time helping the pilots and bombarding them with hosts of questions about this and that instrument or navigational problem and even about the aircraft's engines.

Although she took no real part in the flying of the aircraft. the very fact that she had actually flown the Atlantic made Amelia world-famous almost over-night. She was asked to go on lecture tours of America, telling of her experiences and to write articles for newspapers and magazines, all of which brought her in the money she needed to continue her flying.

But there was more to Amelia's wish to become a better pilot than hopes of short haul trips in America. Spurred on by her Atlantic flight, she determined that one day she would fly the Atlantic again, but this time she would do it alone. At the very suggestion of this, Palmer was staggered. By then his relationship with Amelia had grown into something more than just friendship and he did all in his power to persuade her to forget this foolish venture. But Amelia was made of strong and stubborn stuff. She continued flying until she became a first-class pilot and certainly the match for any man.

As time went by and Amelia gained more and more distinctions by completing long cross-country flights in America, the desire to fulfil her ambition grew. Palmer did all in his power to dissuade her from undertaking the trip but her resolution won the day and in 1931, she declared that she was ready for the flight. Realising that he could never stop her, Palmer at last gave her his blessing, doing everything he could to help her. But before committing himself too far, he asked her to marry him. After due consideration, Amelia accepted his proposal of marriage, but not without certain conditions, which she even went to the extent of putting down in writing! He was in no way to interfere with her flying. A 'beaten man', Palmer agreed to her conditions and they were duly married.

The truth of the matter was that Palmer fully understood Amelia's desire for freedom and need for an ever-present challenge. Palmer had won fame for his courage during two Arctic expeditions which he had undertaken, so the lust for adventure was in him, too.

The following year, 1932, Amelia achieved her dream. She flew solo across the Atlantic in only thirteen and a half hours, shattering a world record and becoming the world's first lady of aviation. The trip was not without its difficulties. Like many others before her she had faced abominable weather, howling gales, fierce rain storms and dense cloud. To make matters worse, her altimeter and petrol gauge had failed, then an exhaust pipe on her Lockheed Monoplane split open and choking fumes and flames crept into the cockpit. Only her superb skill as a pilot and her dogged tenacity brought her through the ordeal.

After her epic flight, the name of Amelia Earhart became a household word. But she determined not to stop there. There were other challenges to overcome, other oceans to cross. She made many more dramatic flights and became an expert on aircraft engines, showing a particular interest in the autogyro the forerunner of the modern-day helicopter. She actually flew the autogyro on several occasions and gave many technical lectures throughout the country.

Amelia Earhart was, above all, determined to show that aviation was not a world exclusively set aside for men. She did all in her power to encourage other women to take up flying....not because she was an ardent advocate of 'women's liberation' but because she wanted other women to experience the thrill of flight as she had done.

In 1935, Amelia once more staggered the world when she flew solo across the Pacific Ocean from Hawaii to California, the first person ever to do so. World records fell to her as the years went by and Amelia kept on with the same resolve she had shown in earlier years. She was aiming for the one achievement which, until then, had eluded her. She wanted to fly right around the world.

This, she promised her husband would be the last long-distance trip she would make. Amelia could not have foreseen then that what she said would come literally true – but in a tragic way.

The route she was to fly from Oakland, California, was to take her across the American continent, down to Brazil, over the South Atlantic to Africa then east across the world, culminating in a flight across the Pacific Ocean. She was to take with her as navigator, one of the most skilled in the business, Fred Noonan.

In 1937, Amelia was presented with a brand new twin-engined Lockheed aircraft for her services to aviation. She christened it *Electra*. It was in this aircraft that she planned to make her round-the-world trip. On the 1st June, 1937, she and Fred Noonan took off from Oakland and the epic adventure began....

In spite of adverse conditions much of the way, the trip round the world to the Pacific Ocean went according to plan. It was this vast expanse of ocean that was to prove the final challenge to Amelia Earhart. The weather alone, as they waited to take off from Lae, in New Guinea, seemed to herald disaster. Their next stop in the hops across the Pacific was to be Howland, a tiny coral island over 2500 miles from Lae. The weather was appalling. From the airstrip which had been hastily cut out of the jungle, they experienced the full force of a Pacific storm. It rained incessantly while thunder boomed and lightning streaked the storm-blackened sky.

While she and Fred waited for the storm to abate, Amelia set about checking their flight plan, provisions and safety equipment for the journey. This was to be the longest single lap of the journey and she was taking every precaution. The vital radio was checked along with the rubber dinghy, Very pistol, signalling lamps, iron rations and the many other things that went to make for a safer trip. Nothing had been left to chance. If they were forced down into the sea, they would have all the equipment necessary for survival.

She wrote to her husband....

'The whole width of the world has passed beneath us, except this broad ocean. I shall be glad when we have the hazard of its navigation behind us.'

It was not until the morning of the 2nd July that the weather brightened and Amelia and Fred could contemplate taking off. The take-off alone presented considerable difficulties for the intrepid aviatrix. The space which had been cleared for a runway was small and further complicated by the towering trees which surrounded it. All Amelia's skill was going to be required to get the fuel-laden aircraft up and over the trees.

The lumbering aircraft trundled along the runway and lifted into the air, barely skimming the tops of the trees then made off into the blue sky dotted with puffy white clouds. The weather for the hop to Howland was reasonable and there seemed to be no problems ahead of them, save for the gargantuan task Fred Noonan had to face in navigating across the vast waste of rolling waves.

The difficulty of navigation was an enormous one but Noonan was equal to the task. He had pioneered the San

Francisco/Manila run for Pan American Airways. If it were humanly possible to navigate across the trackless wastes of ocean, Noonan was the man to do it and he had planned his route for the last leg of the journey with meticulous care.

A coast guard cutter, the *Itasca*, was riding at anchor off Howland with orders to help guide Amelia's aircraft in to the airstrip. The boat was equipped with high-powered radio equipment and capable of transmitting weather information to the *Electra*. The whole schedule of the operation had been worked out in detail. Commander Thompson, the captain of the cutter, was given explicit instructions which were to be followed to the letter. They read:

'Earhart's call letters are K.H.A.Q.Q. Earhart to broadcast her position on 3105 kilocycles at every fifteen and forty-five minutes past the hour. *Itasca* to broadcast weather and homing signal on 3105 and 7500 kilocycles on the hour and half-hour.'

The system seemed without fault and incapable of misinterpretation — but problems were to arise. Something happened to the *Electra* with disastrous consequences....

In the radio cabin of the *Itasca*, the operator tried in vain to contact *Electra* for seven hours after she had left Lae. No reply came. In desperation, Thompson contacted a radio direction finder unit at Howland to see if they had any more promising news but he drew a blank. They had not heard a thing.

At one o'clock in the morning of the 4th July, Thompson put out a call to the coast guard on the Californian coast indicating that he had heard nothing from Amelia but that he was not unduly concerned because according to the schedule they were at that time still 1000 miles away.

Following the message to the coast guard he broadcast to *Electra* the weather conditions which were 'excellent'. Then he waited...and waited... but nothing was heard from Amelia until just before 3 o'clock in the morning, when a faint voice was heard through heavy static on the radio. It was Amelia.

'Encountering headwinds....cloudy and overcast.' Then the voice died out. More messages were transmitted from *Electra* but they were so distorted by static that they were almost unintelligible. Then at 6.15 a.m. Howland time, came the most coherent message of the night.

'We are about 100 miles out. Please take a bearing on us

and report in half an hour. I will transmit in the microphone.'
The message was short and clipped....too short for the
Howland operators to get a proper radio 'fix' on the aircraft.

From then on there was complete silence. In a bid to find
the tiny aircraft, the radio direction finder unit swept the sky
with its beams only to encounter utter silence. As far as they
were concerned, the *Electra* was lost but they were determined not to give up trying and continued the search. Then
came a stroke of luck, Amelia's voice came through with
startling clarity at 7.42....

'We must be right on top of you but we can't see you. Our
gas (petrol) is running low and we've only about thirty
minutes left. Have been unable to reach you by radio. We are
flying at an altitude of 1000 feet. Please take a bearing.' Then
the din of static started up again and Amelia's voice was lost.
Shortly afterwards came yet another message....

'We are circling but still cannot see you! Go ahead on 7500
kilocycles either now or on the scheduled half-hourly time!'

The *Itasca*, at the duly appointed time, transmitted
Amelia's call sign in morse code in the hope that it would not
be affected by static but it was still impossible to get a
bearing. Then Amelia made a transmission....

'We are receiving your signals but we are unable to get a
minimum. Please take a bearing and answer with voice on
3105.'

Not long after, at 8.45, Amelia was heard for the last time.
She said in a weak voice....

'We are in a line of position 157-337, repeat 157-337. Will
repeat this message now on 6210 kilocycles. We are running
north and south. We have only half an hour's fuel left and we
cannot see land.'

Amelia Earhart and Fred Noonan were never heard or seen
again. As the minutes ticked by into hours it was obvious to
all that they had ditched into the sea. But that did not
necessarily mean they were doomed. Everyone hoped that
they had survived the crash and were waiting to be picked up
in their life raft. There was still a chance that they were alive.

It must be remembered that the search procedures in the
1930s were not the elaborate ones they are today. There was,
however, one ray of hope. The fuel tanks of the *Electra*
would be empty and therefore provide considerable
buoyancy for the aircraft. If only the crash landing was

successful then there was a fair chance that they might still be alive, if not in the life raft then waiting on the buoyant wings of the aircraft for rescue. However, a full scale search by ships and aircraft revealed nothing. In spite of attempts by radio 'hams' all around the Pacific coastline, there was no sign of life from Amelia's radio.

A whole string of suspected calls from K.H.A.Q.Q. were heard or reported as having been heard. The most promising of these was...

'We are on a coral reef just below the equator....we are okay but a little weak.'

However, none of the reported messages led to anything. Wild rumours about their fate were rife throughout the world but one particularly sinister one came from the island of Saipan, which lies north of Howland Island. Years later someone on the island, while discussing the mysterious disappearance of Amelia Earhart, remembered an incident which occurred in 1937 when a light aircraft carrying a man and a woman crash landed in the sea just off the island coast. Then another person recalled seeing an aircraft crash land in the sea and a man and woman emerge from it to be arrested by armed Japanese who were at that time building an airstrip on the island. This witness saw the couple taken into the woods by the Japanese and there followed two shots. Nothing more was heard of them. Putting two and two together they surmised that the couple were none other than Amelia and Fred Noonan. But this posed a question. Why should the Japanese murder them out of hand? Was it to hide the fact that they were illegally building an airstrip on the island? If word of that got out there would surely be an international incident. It was a horrific possibility.

The rumours grew to alarmist proportions and there were suggestions that both Amelia and Fred Noonan were in fact American spies who had been using the round-the-world trip to cover up their true mission....to seek out the islands on which the Japanese were carrying out their unlawful work. There are those who, even now, believe that this was the case. It is said that the Japanese military authorities held a complete dossier on Amelia Earhart. Why would they have such a thing on a female flier whose sole interest in life was flying? Could it have been that she was a Japanese spy? There are those who believe this version to be true and also believe that the aircraft she was flying did not crash land but was shot down *by American fighters* to cover up her duplicity!

Knowing of Amelia's love for adventure and the thrill of a challenge, it is not too difficult to believe that she may have been implicated or engaged in spying on behalf of the Americans but the very suggestion that she was in any way connected with the Japanese is too ridiculous to be considered. Amelia Earhart was an American in every sense of the word, loyal and abundantly proud of her country.

Was Amelia Earhart spying or was she, as many hold to be true, killed with Fred Noonan when their aircraft crashed into the sea? Perhaps, somewhere there is hidden the truth but it seems unlikely that the mysterious disappearance of the world's greatest woman pilot will ever be solved.

10
Pioneers from Down Under

Close by the busy runway of Brisbane's Eagle Farm Airport in Queensland, Australia, there stands an impressive structure of glass and timber inside which is housed one of the world's most famous aeroplanes, a three-engined Fokker monoplane. Emblazoned upon its fuselage are the words *Southern Cross*. It stands there as an everlasting tribute to the greatest of all Australia's intrepid poineer aviators, Sir Charles Kingsford-Smith.

Kingsford-Smith, or 'Smithy' as he was, and still is, affectionately known by all Australians, was a man of immense courage and determination. In his lifetime he was to need those qualitites, for it was punctuated with triumph and tragedy the like of which would have ruined lesser men. But even in the face of adversity he maintained the one overriding virtue which was to bring him through some unbelievable tests of human endurance — his sense of humour.

Smithy was born in Brisbane in 1897 and even as a young man he showed a taste for adventure. At the tender age of six, his parents took him for a holiday to Canada and one day, as the ship was ploughing its way across the Pacific Ocean, his horrified mother and father found him hanging by his tiny hands from a hawse hole in the ship's bow, dangling above the heaving seas, illustrating to a friend how this could be done! Many years later he was to risk his life over that same ocean.

However, in the meantime, there came the First World War. In 1915, at the age of fifteen, Smithy enlisted in the Australian infantry and became a dispatch rider. Not long after his basic training was complete he was shipped to the war zone and saw action in Egypt, Gallipoli and France.

It was while he was in the thick of all the action that he caught the flying bug. He saw the frail fighting planes of the Royal Flying Corps soaring through the skies on their way to do battle with the Germans. The thought of wheeling into action against the enemy gripped Smithy's imagination and he volunteered for service in the R.F.C. To his delight he was accepted and commissioned into this service in 1917.

With all the enthusiasm of a determined young man he launched himself into his pilot training and showed that he had a natural aptitude for flying. Every day he flew with his instructor until the time came when he was to take to the air on his own, a harrowing experience even for a man with strong nerves.

With Smithy alone at the controls the aircraft got into the air all right and was soon up at 500 feet. As he banked round in a turn, the thrill of actually flying the aircraft on his own for the first time swept through him. He circled the field then dipped the nose for the landing approach. Down the aircraft came and as he neared the ground, he eased back on the control column lifting the nose slightly to level off for the landing. The grass raced beneath him and he cut the engine, but alas too soon. He had misjudged his height and the aircraft fell out of the sky and hit the grass with a resounding crunch. The fragile machine disintegrated and Smithy was banged and slammed about the cockpit, sustaining some nasty bumps and bruises. Yet miraculously he was not seriously hurt and emerged from the tangle of wreckage with a broad grin on his face. His first solo flight had ended ignominiously but Smithy was undaunted and quick to get into the air again.

In due course, he qualified as a pilot and went to war in earnest, earning himself the Military Cross for his daring. He also earned one other dubious distinction, the loss of three toes which were shot off during a dog-fight.

With the end of the war, Smithy returned to Australia determined to continue flying. While in the R.F.C. he had often thought about what he would do after the war. He thought of his homeland, of its vast expanses of desert, its great mountain ranges and the major cities of Australia, all hundreds and sometimes thousands of miles apart. His country was young and enterprising. It was growing year by year but it lacked the one thing that would enable it to become truly great – fast means of communication between the major centres of industry. There was only one really fast way of moving between these remote places and that was by air.

With this in mind, Smithy set about planning a domestic airline for Australia, one which would link all these places. He visualised a time when the big cities would be within only an hour or so flying time of each other. But all this was a dream. To turn it into reality, Smithy needed money – and lots of it. Above all he had to find backers who would provide the finance to buy the aircraft he required for his venture. No one was interested. Setting up an airline was to be no easy task as he soon found out. Few wealthy Australians were interested in flying in those days and Smithy, in spite of his many other talents, was no business-man. He had seen other airlines fail as quickly as they had begun. For instance there had been the one started by another young Australian, Charles Ulm. After the war he had tried to float a company to operate a passenger service between Sydney and Melbourne but alas, Australian business-men did not share his enthusiasm, and the venture had proved a flop.

Smithy did all he could to raise the money to get his company off the ground but he found that he was fighting a losing battle and it was not until he and Ulm met and decided to pool their resources that the venture looked anything like reaching fruition. In spite of their setbacks the two men had not lost heart and were still charged with enthusiasm for the project. They planned and schemed, doing everything in their power, to get it off the ground. They talked for hours upon end, trying desperately to work out how they could do it.

Then one day, Smithy hit upon an idea. Somehow or other they had to prove to the financiers that the aeroplane was here to stay. They had to do something dramatic; something that would make all Australia sit up and take notice – they had to do something no one else had ever done before.

It did not take the two men long to agree upon their goal – the Pacific Ocean. Until then no man had succeeded in flying across this vast ocean, the widest in the world. What an achievement it would be if they could become the first to do so. What a sensation it would cause. Surely after such an achievement, the big businessmen from all over the world would flock to invest in their company. That would be, of course, *after* they had succeeded. For the time being they had to raise money to buy an aircraft in which to undertake their dare-devil flight. But whatever the cost they were determined to do it and they poured every penny they had between them into the venture.

Since they had met with little success among the business-men in Australia they decided to sail to the United States to try their luck there. Once in America they used all their persuasive powers and succeeded in raising the money to buy an aircraft. With the money they had accumulated they bought a three-engined Fokker high-winged monoplane which they christened the *Southern Cross*.

The Fokker was an unattractive aircraft and had an almost 'awkward' look about it, but it was a sturdy machine and had proved its reliability by taking Sir Hubert Wilkins to the Arctic during his explorations there. The sceptics amongst those who learned of Smithy's project reckoned that the aircraft would never leave the ground with a crew of four and heavily laden with all the fuel that was required for the trip, but Smith and Ulm refused to be deterred. They had come this far and they certainly were not giving up now.

Smithy enlisted two other men to join the crew. They were both Americans, Harry Lyon, the navigator, and James Warner, the radio operator.

On the appointed day, May the 31st, 1928, the four men climbed aboard the *Southern Cross* at Oakland, California, under the gaze of an awe-struck crowd which encircled the plane. Minutes later, after Smithy completed the pre-flight checks, each engine in turn burst into life and the aircraft moved slowly to the take-off point at the end of the runway.

Smithy wheeled the aircraft round into wind and eased the throttles forward. The engines roared in a deafening crescendo of sound, then Smithy released the brake and the Fokker slowly rolled forward, gathering speed as it went. For what seemed like an eternity, the aircraft's wheels clung to the ground with the weight holding her down. In the cockpit, Smithy's eyes flashed from the scene before him to the panel of instruments. The needle on the speed indicator seemed reluctant to reach the take-off speed and they were fast running out of runway, but at last it crept up to the mark and Smithy eased back on the control column. Obediently, but with great reluctance, the Fokker rose from the ground. *Southern Cross* was on its way at last. Before it lay almost eight thousand miles of open sea with scattered tiny islands dotted about it. Above all else perfect navigation was vital, for if they missed their stopping-off points across the ocean, there would be no second chance.

All four men aboard that small aircraft knew only too well the hazards they might face. Unlike today, when meteorologists can warn pilots of bad weather they are likely to encounter over the oceans, there was no way in Smithy's day of predicting the weather. Improvisation was the key word and Smithy was to need every ounce of it during this journey. Time after time he and Ulm had to alter course by many miles to avoid storms. Their aircraft could not fly above the weather as the jet liners of today can, so they had to deviate from their set course to avoid disaster and in so doing they taxed every ounce of their navigator's skill.

Should anything happen to them while they were far out over the ocean they had almost no hope at all of rescue. The massive search and rescue operations which are mounted today when an aircraft is reported missing were impossible in Smithy's day, and each one of them knew it. But in spite of this ever-present thought they flew on across the seemingly endless expanse of heaving sea.

Their Fokker aircraft could not have been less comfortable. The four men were cramped in the small cockpit with the constant roar of the engines drumming in their ears and the biting wind whistling through every crevice in the fuselage, adding to the already unpleasant sensation of almost continuous buffeting by strong wind.

By some near miraculous feat of navigation, Harry Lyon succeeded in leading Smithy across the trackless wastes of sea. Then came the longest haul of all, to the Fiji Islands, some three thousand miles from their last port of call at Honolulu in the Hawaiian Islands. The weather was abominable. Howling gale-force winds made worse by driving rain tossed the Fokker about the sky like so much match-wood while Smithy and Charles Ulm fought with the controls to keep the plane in the sky.

For *thirty-three* hours they kept that aircraft airborne until there, on the horizon was their goal, the Fiji Islands. They were all absolutely exhausted but jubilant at their success in getting so far. Smithy circled the Fijian capital of Suva for a suitable place to land and spotted the Albert Park, the only available open space. A closer inspection of this stretch of grass showed it to be far from the perfect touch-down area. It was bumpy and ringed with tall trees and high telegraph wires. But with their fuel running out and no alternative place in sight he had little choice other than to make the attempt.

If Smithy was to succeed in the limited space available he would almost have to drop the Fokker onto the ground immediately he cleared the trees. Down he went on the approach and just as the Fokker skimmed over the trees, he cut the engine and laid the plane on the ground but he had no sooner done so than he realised that he would never be able to stop the aircraft in time to avoid smashing into the trees at the far end of the park. The Fokker sped on towards the towering trees. As it thundered on over the uneven grass, the vast trees became enormous towering giants before their eyes. Smithy hauled on the brakes but still the plane thundered on. He had to act fast or they were doomed. There was only one thing to do — swerve.

Smithy jammed forward the starboard throttle and the engine screamed as it reached full power, then he kicked the left rudder. In an instant the aircraft wheeled round to the left missing the trees by only a few feet but in so doing the port wing-tip bit into the ground and the aircraft shuddered to a halt amid a billowing cloud of dust. Smithy instantly cut the engines and all four men clambered out, shaken but in one piece, to survey the damage.

To their astonishment, the damage was slight. The

momentary thought that their journey had come to a permanent end was swept from their minds. Still, from then on it was all hands to the pump in an effort to get the Fokker into working shape again. After hours of toil she was ready to take to the air, but not before Smithy had insisted on some of the locals chopping down a few of the trees at the end of his 'runway'.

Finally, after a path had been cleared for take-off, *Southern Cross* once more took to the air and Smithy set off on the final leg of the epic flight. At last, on June 9th, *Southern Cross* touched down on a dusty track which is now Eagle Farm Airport, Brisbane. Utterly exhausted but triumphant the four men emerged from their plane, the first to conquer the Pacific. The trans-oceanic flight had taken them nine days with a total flying time of eighty-three hours.

All Australia hailed them as heroes, and banner headlines in the newspapers of the world proclaimed their bravery. As Smithy had predicted, there was a flood of money, some £20,000 in all, subscribed to foot the bill for other flights. These flights were a challenge. There were other routes across the world which had at that time not been conquered and the temptation to launch himself into these was difficult for Smithy to resist. He could not forget the reason why he and Ulm had embarked upon their Pacific flight in the first place – to raise money for the formation of an Australian airline.

Smithy and Charles Ulm were to make more record-breaking flights but not before they had got their airline off the ground. Now that they were famous, the businessmen, who in the past had chosen to write their schemes off as hairbrained, were now more willing to listen. They succeeded in raising enough money to form their own company, Australian National Airways Ltd. At last, they thought, they would achieve what they had hoped for for so long but, alas, it seemed that fate was against them.

True, they went on to achieve some truly remarkable 'firsts' in pioneering flight, most of them carried out in the faithful *Southern Cross*. They made the first Sydney, Australia, to Croydon, England, flight in 1929. The following year Smithy broke the light aircraft solo record between England and Australia. Then in 1932 the first official Australia-England airmail flight. Later that year another

Australia-England flight when Smithy went alone. Two years later Smithy smashed the record once more on the England-Australia run, completing the trip in seven days, four hours and forty-four minutes. And finally in 1934 came the first West East Pacific flight in a Lockheed Altair. All of these were staggering feats in themselves and for them Smithy was knighted.

But while Smithy and Ulm met with such success in these remarkable achievements, their airline company was on a disaster course.

When the A.N.A. was first formed, Smithy and Ulm bought the latest Avro Fokker aircraft to start their fleet. They opened offices both in Melbourne and Sydney and built modern hangars at Mascot, staffed by some of the finest aircraft mechanics in Australia. They recruited pilots who had already proved themselves to be first-rate men. They set high standards and wanted nothing but the best. Ulm trained and tested his pilots until they had reached perfection. But even from the beginning, there were to be major setbacks.

The first came not long after they had formed their new company when, in April 1929, the two men set off in *Southern Cross* on a business trip to England. Shortly after they took off they flew headlong into a blinding storm and had to make an emergency landing in the Kimberley region of Western Australia. Without radio or any other means of warning anyone of their plight, they were in a perilous situation. All they could do was sit tight and hope that they would be found by search parties sent out to look for them. For *twelve days* they waited until they were eventually rescued, but although they survived the ordeal, two of the fliers who set out to find them were killed when their aircraft crashed. This tragedy brought bitter criticism from those who believed those pioneering flights to be foolhardy adventures, and the weight of public opinion turned against Smithy and his partner. The resulting adverse publicity hurt their newly-formed airline badly.

As if that were not enough, another disaster was to follow; one which was to result in one of the world's most famous air mysteries.

On a cold, blustery morning in March 1931. 'Shorty' Shortridge, the thirty-three-year-old chief pilot of Australian National Airways, climbed aboard the gleaming blue and silver three engined Avro Fokker airliner *Southern Cloud*, the pride of the A.N.A. fleet. Moments later he was joined by Charlie Dunnell, his co-pilot and the six passengers who were to make the 450 mile trip from Mascot Aerodrome, Sydney, to Melbourne.

The weather that morning was bad but to two skilled pilots like Shortridge and Dunnell, nothing to give rise to concern. Both of them had flown in much worse conditions, probing their way, flying 'blind' by instruments, through murky skies.

In due course, the aircraft's engines roared into life and *Southern Cloud* took off. The flight that lay ahead of them was to take them over the Australian Alps, wild rugged peaks which formed a forbidding barrier between Sydney and Melbourne where some of the worst weather in all the continent was to be found. Neither man, however, was unduly worried at the hazard that lay ahead of them. They had both made the same flight many times before and knew the country over which they were to fly like the backs of their hands.

While *Southern Cloud* droned south west, alarming news reached Mascot Aerodrome. The Sydney weather bureau issued a report warning of the most unbelievably bad conditions waiting for *Southern Cloud* on its course. Howling gales, thunderstorms and torrential rain were creating almost suicidal conditions in the sky on their path to Melbourne. Smithy and Ulm were horrified when they heard the news, all the more so because, without radio contact with the plane, they had no means of warning Shortridge of the danger. They both prayed that Shorty would be able to make it to one of the refuelling airfields before he got caught up in the aerial turmoil.

Wasting no time they warned the people at the refuelling point to keep a sharp look out for *Southern Cloud* and let Mascot Aerodrome know immediately the aeroplane was sighted. All day they waited anxiously but no news came of *Southern Cloud*. Their worst fears had been realised. *Southern Cloud* was missing. She had been forced down somewhere and the burning question was – where? There were countless hundreds of square miles of desolate country where no man had ever set foot. There were rugged mountain peaks and vast expanses of forest so dense that the likelihood of finding an aircraft amongst it was minimal. *Southern Cloud* could have come down anywhere in that treacherous countryside.

Smithy and Ulm got their heads together trying desperately to figure out where the aircraft was likely to be. They tried to work out all the various permutations of what could have happened to it given the prevailing wind and storm conditions. With the violent storms which had prevailed over the course the aircraft had taken they had to allow for it having been blown many miles off course.

Nothing could be done that night so Smithy and Ulm had to wait until the morning before mustering as many aircraft as they could to mount the search. Even before they climbed into their aircraft, dozens of anxious relatives and friends of the passengers on *Southern Cloud* were crowding into the A.N.A. offices. Volunteers to help in the search poured in. Some of them were private pilots and others from the Royal Australian Air Force. Plane after plane took off to scour the country north east of Victoria, which at that time seemed the most likely spot for the disaster to have occurred.

The search itself was fraught with hazard and danger. If the searchers were to have even a remote chance of spotting the stricken aircraft they would have to fly below the towering peaks of the Australian Alps, where great banks of thick mist clung to the valleys. Hidden in these swirling mists were untold dangers.

Smithy himself picked the most inhospitable of all the areas to search, the Strathbogie Ranges. He took fantastic risks, skimming tree tops, sweeping along sheer cliffs and hurtling down deep mist-shrouded valleys, all in a bid to catch sight of *Southern Cloud*. Yet he could find nothing, and neither could any of the other searchers.

For ten days the search continued with Smithy and Ulm working day and night. By then over 100,000 square miles of territory had been scoured without success and it was with a heavy heart that the two pioneer aviators had to admit there was no longer any hope of the passengers and crew of *Southern Cloud* being found alive. The search was called off.

The tragedy of the *Southern Cloud* spelt doom for Smithy's airline and only three months later the company had to be disbanded. Smithy and Ulm were desolated but with the fighting spirit that was common to both of them they went on to achieve even greater things in the air. But alas these too were to result in tragedy for both of them as will be seen.

One question seemed left unanswered — what had happened to *Southern Cloud*? Smithy and Ulm were never to know, for the mystery was solved years later after both of them were dead; in fact twenty-seven years to be precise and even then it was only by a freak chance that the truth of what had happened came to light.

In 1958 work was going on to divert Australia's most famous river, the Snowy, in the construction of a mighty waterway to supply water where it was desperately needed for irrigation. The project was a vast undertaking and many hundreds of men were brought into that area of the continent to work on the scheme. One of these men was a carpenter called Thomas Sonter. He was working in the Toolong Mountains and on Sunday, the 26th October, 1958, he had a day off so, being a keen photographer, he decided to go a walk in the mountains and take a few photographs to add to his collection. He wandered amongst the close-knit trees with their high canopies of branches between whose leaves the sunlight barely managed to filter.

It was while he was tramping through this 'hidden world' that he caught sight of a tangle of twisted metal in amongst some young saplings. His curiosity got the better of him and he struggled through the young trees and tugged at the metal, pulling some of it from the deep grass. As he did so he unearthed more. Pulling the grass aside he discovered that he was actually standing on top of a great pile of steel. Because of its wrecked condition he was puzzled as to what it could be. His excitement grew as he gathered all the bits and pieces he could carry and rushed off down the mountain to his camp.

Back at the camp, speculation grew as to what he had discovered but everyone realised that without expert help they could not throw any light on the mysterious objects. The authorities were informed and in no time at all the Department of Civil Aviation was called in and a group of experts made their way to the spot where Sonter had found the wreckage. When they got there they quickly realised what they had found....the remains of *Southern Cloud*. To confirm their find, they unearthed an identification disc which positively identified the plane as one which had gone missing twenty-seven years before. The skeletal bodies of the passengers and crew were found along with personal items they had carried which had not already been eroded by the weather.

The experts dug and sifted through what they found, trying to piece everything together so that they could solve the mystery of why and how the tragedy had occurred. From what they could gather by the position of the aircraft and the damage to the wings, fuselage and undercarriage, they were able to determine that the aircraft had been in a level turn when it hit the ridge. It was also clear from the force of the impact that the pilot had not been trying to crash land but had in fact flown headlong into the ridge unaware that it was there.

From the position of the wreck, it was plain that Shorty Shortridge had been blown some sixteen miles off his intended course. What happened then no one will ever know for sure and the reason for the tragedy still remains one of aviation's greatest unsolved mysteries.

In spite of the tragedy, the irrepressible Smithy and Ulm were to continue flying in the true pioneering spirit. Both of them were determined to re-establish themselves in the airline business, but in doing so both of them met their deaths in mysterious circumstances.

Charles Ulm's ambition was to establish an air mail service between Australia and America. Using all his powers of persuasion, he managed to scrape together enough money to buy a brand-new Airspeed Envoy aeroplane, a twin-engined low-wing monoplane, which he named *Stella Australis.* Buoyant with enthusiasm he carried out exhaustive tests on the aircraft in the United States and found that it handled perfectly. With boundless enthusiasm he set about modifying the aircraft for the long journey to Australia and after yet more tests, he and his crew were ready to begin their epic flight on the 4th December, 1933. Early that morning they took off from the airfield at Oakland, California, the same one from which five years earlier Ulm and Smithy had made their first Pacific flight.

Once airborne, Ulm set course for Honolulu, the first stopping-off point. At 10.30 a.m., he reported by radio that all was going well, then again at midday a message was received from him that he was progressing even better than expected.

They flew on through the night and early the following morning, when they were well past the half-way point between Oakland and Honolulu, Ulm called up Honolulu on the radio for a forecast of weather conditions on the island. It was shortly after that that the trouble began. Not only were they flying in darkness, they met with dense cloud and had to rely entirely on their directional instruments for guidance through it.

At 7.30 a.m. the controllers at Honolulu heard the worst. Ulm reported that he was lost and fast running out of fuel. Desperately he tried to make a landfall, groping his way through the dense cloud while the precious fuel was drunk up by the thirsty engines. The needles on the fuel gauges crept round to empty and frantic S.O.S. signals were flashed out from *Stella Australis*. Then at 9.23 a.m. came the final tragic news,

'Going down in sea. Plane will float. Come and get us!'

Those few words were the last ever heard from Ulm. In spite of a massive air and sea search, nothing was found of the stricken plane or its crew. Australia had lost one of its two finest airmen. Before long it was to lose the other.....

Smithy, like his compatriot Ulm, tried desperately to open new mail routes across the world but he tried in vain. His attempts were dogged by misfortune. Then on the 6th November, 1935, Smithy took off from Lympe in Kent with Tommy Pethybridge as co-pilot in an aircraft he had christened *Lady Southern Cross*. He was aiming to make the England-Australia trip in record time but alas fate was to play a cruel hand in this flight....

All went well on the flight as far as Allahabad, which they reached in record time beating the previous record by three hours. Smithy was optimistic that they could cut the time by quite a considerable margin. In fact he was so confident that he cabled Sydney and told them to expect him by midnight on the 8th November. Shortly after, Smithy took off again and only a few hours later, his aircraft was seen by another Australian flier over the Bay of Bengal. That was the last anyone ever saw of *Lady Southern Cross* and Charles Kingsford-Smith. What became of the intrepid aviator no one will ever know, but one theory is that the aircraft was struck by lightning, a not uncommon occurrence in that part of the world.

Australia had lost both of her most famous fliers; the two men who had done more than anyone else to put that vast continent in the forefront of civil aviation and point the way for the great Australian airmen of today.

11
The Battle of Britain

In the late 1930s an uneasy peace existed in Europe. Throughout the years that had followed the First World War, Adolf Hitler, fanatical German nationalist and leader of the Nazi party, planned revenge on the countries which had brought about Germany's downfall.

Secretly he and one of his lieutenants, Hermann Goering, a World War One fighter ace and one-time leader of the famous Richthofen squadron, set about building up the German Luftwaffe, which was to become the most powerful air force in the world.

By 1939, Hitler's armed forces were ready to march and on September the 2nd of that year, the entire might of the German Army, backed up by the Luftwaffe, smashed its way into Poland, crushing the meagre resistance that lay in its path. In spite of the fact that she was ill-prepared, Britain honoured the defence treaty she had with Poland and the following day the Prime Minister declared war on Germany. For the second time in less than a quarter of a century, a desperate struggle was about to begin with Germany.

Hitler's lightning attack on Poland left the country in ruins and after a few months he was ready to mount a full-scale attack on the west. With the same speed, Holland and Belgium fell and soon it was France's turn to meet the onrushing might of the 'master race'.

By then a British Expeditionary Force was already in France. Terrible battles raged in which the British and French forces fought with supreme gallantry but it was soon clear that Germany's superbly-equipped and highly-mobile forces were winning the day. The Allies were forced back towards the sea and were saved from complete annihilation only by a brilliant sea-borne rescue operation at Dunkirk. Now the shattered remnants of the B.E.F. could act as the nucleus of future armies forming in Britain. They had lost a battle but not the war and, with typical British resolve, they determined that one day they would return to continental Europe and crush the Nazi menace once and for all.

Following the British defeat in France, Goering, the Commander-in-Chief of the Luftwaffe, began a bomber offensive against Britain, sending over 70-strong formations in night attacks on R.A.F. airfields and aircraft factories. These nocturnal raids were small in comparison with what was to come but they were intended to give the Luftwaffe experience of flying and navigating over the British Isles at night. The Royal Air Force, seriously ill-equipped and under-manned through lack of fighters and trained pilots, put up what defence it could but it was no match for the highly-organised Luftwaffe. Goering, encouraged by the Luftwaffe's successes during its continental campaign, saw the forthcoming battle with the R.A.F. as a 'push-over' and indeed, boasted that he could crush the British air force within a few days, and 'bring Britain to her knees'. In July 1940 Hitler named the day for the invasion of Britain. Code-named 'Operation Sealion', the invasion of the British Isles was to take place on the 15th September. Hitler issued a directive to Goering which read:

'The Luftwaffe is to overcome the British Air Force with all the means at its disposal — and as soon as possible'.

The Battle of Britain was about to begin and Britain's chances of surviving the impending onslaught seemed slim. Indeed it appeared that Goering's boast was to come true.

At first glance the odds appeared to weigh heavily against the island nation. Germany had the largest and strongest air force in the world, with over 3000 aircraft, 1100 of which were fighters. Against this formidable aerial armada, the R.A.F. could put up only 600 Spitfire and Hurricane fighters and a few obsolete Boulton Paul Defiants.

On paper it looked as if the R.A.F. would be fighting a battle which it could not win, but the situation was not quite as hopeless as it appeared. The German bomber force was not as strong as it seemed. The Junkers 87 single-engined dive bomber (known as the Stuka) was slow and highly vulnerable to fighter attack as were the other bombers, the Junkers 88, the Heinkel 111, the Dornier 215 and the Dornier 17 (known as the flying pencil because of its long fuselage).

None of these bombers was capable of carrying a really effective bomb-load and one which could deal a crushing blow to the R.A.F's fighter bases. In addition, the bombers needed fighter protection, but because of the German fighter's short range this protection was not as efficient as it should have been.

To protect its bombers, the Luftwaffe had the fast Messerschmitt Bf 109 (known as the *Emil* to the German pilots who flew them) and the twin-engined Messerschmitt 110. The 109 and the Spitfire were almost equals in the air but, although the 109 had a faster rate of climb, the Spitfire could easily out-manoeuvre it. In addition the 109 had a limited range of 100 miles and an operating time of only 20 minutes over Southern England. The 110 had a greater range but was comparatively slow and sluggish and proved a fairly easy target for the British fighters.

The Hurricane, Britain's first monoplane fighter was powered by a Rolls Royce Merlin engine and had a speed of 328 m.p.h. It was armed with eight .303 machine-guns but was no match for the 109 and was generally reserved for the job of bomber interception.

Without doubt, the Spitfire was the finest fighter on either side. With its Rolls Royce Griffon engine it had a top speed of 360 m.p.h. It was superbly manoeuvrable and could run rings round anything the Germans could put in the air. As well as its great agility it had the hitting power of eight rapid-fire Browning machine-guns mounted in its wings which could out-gun the 109.

It can be seen therefore that the Luftwaffe was not quite as powerful in the air as many historians would have us believe. Sheer weight of numbers alone would not win the Battle of Britain – as Goering was soon to find to his cost.

Apart from the fact that they would be fighting over home ground, the British had two secret weapons which were to play a decisive part in the battle that was to come. The first was radar. This was an early warning system which had been invented in 1935 by Sir Robert Watson-Watt, a British scientist. He had discovered that radio waves bounced back from the Heavyside Layer of the atmosphere. With this knowledge he invented a device which could bounce a sound wave off an approaching aircraft and send it back to a receiver. In this way the device was able to calculate the height and distance of the oncoming aircraft. It doesn't take much imagination to appreciate how important radar was to become for British pilots. Unlike their predecessors in the First World War, they could be alerted well in advance of an attack and be in the air and waiting for the raiders with the advantage of height and surprise on their side.

Britain's other secret weapon was a bustling, energetic little Canadian man, Lord Beaverbrook, who because of his eagerness for hard work soon got the nickname 'The Beaver'. He had come from Canada and built up the giant *Daily Express* newspaper empire. He was a brilliant organiser and a man who had an uncanny knack of getting what he wanted. Winston Churchill, by then the British Prime Minister, knew him well and appointed him Minister of Aircraft Production. The Beaver threw himself into the job with all the energy he could muster to build up Britain's fighter strength. He worked day and night in his office, snatching only a few hours' sleep in the specially prepared room next to his office. His energy and resource knew no bounds and he thought nothing of telephoning high-ranking officers or politicians in the middle of the night to ask a favour or get the answer to an urgent question. His persuasive powers were so effective that, shortly after taking office, the production of fighters in Britain soared from 200 to 500 a month. But fighters were useless without skilled pilots to fly them and the R.A.F. had only a few of these. Try as it might, the R.A.F. could not train pilots to keep pace with the production of fighters.

Across the length and breadth of Britain the threat of

invasion hung like a black cloud over the population. The memory of World War One German terror raids was still fresh in the minds of many grown-ups and they feared for the safety of their children. There followed a mass evacuation of children from all the major cities in the land. Britain began digging. Air raid shelters were built. Anti-aircraft emplacements sprang up in the most unlikely places, on golf courses, tennis courts and in parks. Lakes were booby-trapped with great lengths of wire stretched across them to prevent seaplanes from landing. A blackout was imposed, plunging the country into darkness. The 'Dad's Army' of the day, the Local Defence Volunteers, later to become known as the Home Guard, carried out patrols, armed with a primitive assortment of weapons ranging from pitch forks to axe handles. Throughout the country posters on walls warned of possible lurking spies and the danger of careless talk. Factories which had been producing peace-time luxury goods were transformed almost overnight to aircraft and munitions production. The fear of gas attack was rife throughout the land and every man, woman and child was issued with a gas mask.

That then was the situation when, on the 13th August, 1940, the greatest aerial clash ever to take place, began. The world's most powerful air force had marshalled its bombers to begin the offensive. That day the German bomber crews boarded their aircraft and took off from several airfields in Holland. The early morning was cloudy and overcast but the Germans, filled with optimism, flew on towards England, chanting their war hymns as they nosed across the Channel towards the White Cliffs of Dover.

The Germans' spirits were high but they were soon to be dashed. Field Marshal Kesselring, the Luftwaffe commander in Holland, had sent an urgent message to the Dutch bomber bases, calling off the raids because of the bad weather, but the warning had arrived too late to stop the bombers. They thundered on towards the English coast unaware of what lay in store for them.

As the vast formations of German aircraft swept over the coast a mass of white blips appeared on the British radar screens. At Fighter Command headquarters in Uxbridge, Air Chief Marshal Park, commander of Number 11 Fighter Group, watched the course of the enemy bombers being plotted on the huge table map in the operations room. He quickly ordered three squadrons of Spitfires and Hurricanes into the air and the battle commenced.

The British fighters plunged into the German formations, raking the enemy with fire. A horde of Stuka bombers was chased back across the Channel by a squadron of Hurricanes from Tangmere airfield.

Under determined attacks by Spitfires, whole formations were broken up into a chaotic jumble over south-east England. One formation of Dorniers did, however, succeed in getting through and bombed the airfield at Eastchurch in Essex. But the weight and ferocity of the R.A.F. attack sent the Germans scurrying home at full throttle.

'Eagle Day', as the Germans called that first day of the battle, was a disaster for the Luftwaffe. One thousand German aircraft had taken part in the raids. Forty-five of these aircraft fell to British guns while the R.A.F. lost only thirteen. Goering was beside himself with rage and urged his crews on to take all sorts of risks to smash the R.A.F., but 'round one' of the desperate fight unquestionably went to the R.A.F.

On the day that followed, a twenty-three year old R.A.F. pilot showed the Luftwaffe what British fighter pilots were made of in an historic encounter which lives on today as an example of the courage of these brave young men.

Flight Lieutenant Nicholson, a flight commander with No. 249 Squadron, was leading a flight of Hurricanes on a routine patrol near Southampton. His alert eyes swept the clear blue sky, searching for intruders but all seemed peaceful. Then suddenly he caught sight of three black dots in the sky ahead of him. He rammed open his throttle and the Hurricane surged forward. As he closed in on the dots they gradually took the shape of three JU 88 bombers. With two other Hurricanes of his squadron hot on his heels, he dashed towards the bombers but just as he was about to fire, a 'posse' of Spitfires pounced as if from nowhere, on the Germans. In only a few seconds, the enemy machines were plunging out of control towards the sea.

Nicholson cursed his luck as he turned the Hurricane's nose to rejoin his flight. But as he made his quick dash back, a pair of German eyes were fixed on his aircraft. A Bf 109 was on his tail and bearing down fast. In a flash Nicholson's canopy disintegrated as cannon shells ripped into the aircraft. The Hurricane shuddered under the fusillade of fire as shells tore into its engine cowling. In seconds, searing flames licked over the whole aircraft and thick, black oily smoke filled the cockpit. Nicholson, hit in the head and with blood streaming over his eyes, was half blinded and choking as his lungs filled with smoke. He could barely see out of one eye.

He pushed his stick to starboard and the 109 screeched past in a steep dive. In spite of his injuries, Nicholson's one thought was to get even with the German. Through a blurred, grey haze he could just see the fuzzy shape of the Messerschmitt. The shadowy outline of the German aircraft moved momentarily into Nicholson's gunsight — just long enough for him to jab the firing button. His eight machine-guns burst into life and sent a cone of fire into the 109. Nicholson's aircraft hugged the tail of the German fighter which plummeted headlong towards the sea at 400 miles an hour. Seconds later it hit the waves and disintegrated.

Nicholson hauled back on the control column and levelled off. The cockpit was now filled with flames. In the heat of battle he had not noticed that the control column and throttle had become white hot. The palms of his hands were sizzling and stuck to the controls. He pulled them free and prepared to bale out. The pain was agonising as he fought to undo his seat straps with his blistered and burnt hands. In desperation he wrenched the belts free and leapt out of the roaring furnace in his cockpit.

The cold air cut into Nicholson's burns like a razor. He dropped through the air with his hands groping for the release ring to pull his parachute open. His scorched hands found it and, bracing himself for the pain, he jerked it. The silk parachute canopy billowed out of its pack and seconds later, there was a comforting *crack* as it opened above him. Gently he floated down towards the sea....but suddenly death lurked nearby. Another 109 roared in towards him. With his senses dulled by excruciating pain, Nicholson peered towards the German aircraft. He had heard gruesome stories of how German pilots had shot down British airmen dangling from their parachutes. Nicholson let his body fall limp, feigning death and the 109 swept passed him and peeled off towards France. His ruse had worked.

Miraculously, Nicholson survived his ordeal, and for his

courage in pressing home the attack, was awarded the Victoria Cross, the only one to be given to a fighter pilot during the Battle of Britain.

The pressure on the R.A.F. fighter pilots as German bombers swept across the Channel and the North Sea in their hundreds was unrelenting. Wave after wave of Dornier and Heinkel bombers, with Messerschmitt fighters buzzing like hornets above them, attacked factories, docks and airfields. Every morning around 9.0 a.m. they would appear and keep coming, unloading their cargoes of death and destruction. Then at 5.0 p.m. the raids would stop. The times of these raids soon came to be known as 'office hours', and during 'office hours' fighter pilots were almost continually in the air, courting death in the bitter dog-fights over southern England. It was a mere handful of young men from a variety of backgrounds – many still in their teens – who had to assume the terrible responsibility for their country's very existence. They and the men and women who kept their aircraft in fighting trim by working almost round the clock saved the day, when Britain had no other effective defence.

Under the tremendous pressures of those days the transformation from a 'green', newly qualified pilot to a veteran often took place in just a few hours. For many of these men their war was a short one and death came quickly. At the end of 'office hours' familiar faces would be missing from the mess. They learned to live, not by the day but by the hour and the minute.

The clang of the alarm bell and the call of 'Squadron scramble' sent them running to their fighters to take off and do battle with the enemy. Often, with one dog-fight over they would dash back to their bases to refuel and re-arm before taking off again almost immediately to face another onslaught. It was not unusual for a pilot to fly five or six sorties in a day. Yet, amazingly, it seemed as if the R.A.F. was gaining the upper hand. By 18th August, the Luftwaffe had lost the staggering number of 236 aircraft to the R.A.F's 95. It was then that Prime Minister Winston Churchill uttered the immortal words of his testimonial to the bravery and courage of these gallant men.

'Never in the field of human conflict has so much been owed by so many to so few!'

The conflict raged on. Airfields were pitted and scarred by

the weight of the Luftwaffe's bombs; aircraft under repair were wrecked on the ground, hangars blasted to bits, control towers put out of action and many R.A.F. ground personnel killed. Many airfields soon became unserviceable. In spite of the R.A.F's victories in the air, the German air force was getting to its targets.

The battles in the air were fast and furious. Sergeant R.F. Hamlyn (later Squadron Leader Hamlyn) described in a B.B.C. broadcast one day's experiences.

'We were up at a quarter past four. I felt in my bones that it was going to be a good day. We were in the air just after five o'clock. Shortly before half past eight we were in the air again looking for enemy raiders approaching the south coast from France. We saw three or four waves of JU 88s protected by a bunch of Bf 109s above them. We were flying at fifteen thousand feet between the bombers and the fighters. The fighters didn't have much chance to interfere with us before we attacked the bombers. I attacked one of the waves of bombers from behind and above. I selected the end bomber of the formation which numbered between fifteen and eighteen. I gave this Junkers a burst of fire which lasted only two seconds but it was enough. It broke away from the formation and dived down, and I saw it crash into the sea. I then throttled back so that I would not overtake the whole formation. I was getting a lot of crossfire from the other bombers as it was, although none of it hit me. If I had broken away after shooting down the first bomber, I should have exposed myself to the full force of the enemy formation's cross-fire, so I throttled back and stayed behind them. I didn't have time to select another bomber target, for almost immediately a Messerschmitt 109 came diving after me. As I throttled back the 109 simply came along and presented me with a beautiful target. He pulled up about 150 yards in front of me so I pressed the gun button for two seconds. He immediately began to smoke and dived away. I followed him this time and saw him go straight into the sea. When the sky was clear of German planes we went home for breakfast. We had a nice "bag" in that combat before the other Germans escaped.

'As a matter of fact I didn't get any breakfast at all. I only had time for a hot drink before we were ordered to stand by again and by half past eleven that morning we were patrolling the south-east coast. We were attacked by half a dozen Bf 109s and of course we broke up to deal with them individually. I had a dog-fight with one, both of us trying to get into a position to deliver an attack but I out-manoeuvred him. I got on his tail and he made off for the French coast as hard as he could. The fight started at ten thousand feet and we raced across the Channel like mad. As we were going like that I saw one of our fellows shoot down another Bf 109 so I said to myself: "I must keep the squadron's average and get this one." I didn't fire at him until we were actually over the French coast, then I let him have it — three nice bursts of fire lasting three seconds each, which, as you may imagine, is an awfully long time. I started that final burst at 8,000 feet and then he began to go down and I followed him until I saw him crash into a field in France. Then I went back home without seeing any enemy at all. I carefully examined my Spitfire when I landed, certain that I must have been hit somewhere. But no, not a mark. It was very satisfactory.

'Our third show began just before four o'clock in the afternoon. We were flying towards the Thames Estuary at 5000 feet when we saw anti-aircraft shells bursting in the sky to the north-east. We changed course and began to climb for the place we thought we should meet the enemy. We did. They were flying at 12,000 feet, twenty JU 88s in tight formation accompanied by about twenty 109s above them. They were flying towards the London area and we could see the balloons shining in the sun. When we spotted the fighters we pulled up towards them. I got under one 109 and gave him two bursts. Smoke started to pour out of him as he went down out of control. Suddenly tracer bullets started whizzing past my machine. I turned sharply and saw a 109 attacking one of our pilots. I turned on the attacker and gave him a quick burst. Immediately he began to slow down and the aircraft began to smoke. I pressed the gun button a second time and the Messerschmitt caught fire. I fired a third time and the whole machine became enveloped in flames and pieces began to fly off. Finally as it went down, more pieces came off, all burning. As it tumbled towards the Thames Estuary it was really a bunch of blazing fragments instead of a whole aircraft. It was an amazing sight. This was my fifth for the day and the squadron's ninety-ninth....'

(Hamlyn's final score at the end of the war was thirteen

confirmed kills).

The sad truth, however, was that Hamlyn's successes were not typical. There was a sudden reversal of success for Fighter Command and R.A.F. losses began to mount at an alarming rate. The battle was swinging in favour of the Luftwaffe which was penetrating Britain's fighter defences and hitting hard at airfields. Biggin Hill, in Kent, was almost razed to the ground. It was hit so hard that for a whole week only one squadron could operate from it. Goering was rubbing his hands with glee. Then on the night of the 24/25th August, the Luftwaffe made its greatest mistake of the war....it attacked London.

On that night, a 200-strong force of German bombers droned over London and unloaded its bombs on the houses below. It has been claimed that this was due to a navigational error and that they had never intended to hit the Metropolis. Buildings crumbled under the weight of the aerial onslaught. Fires raged through houses and firemen fought a desperate and gallant fight to stem the raging inferno. Amid the tumbling masonry men, women and children died. Then dawn revealed the devastation and the dead were counted. All Britain was enraged and shouting for revenge. Churchill was swift to act. That very night a force of R.A.F. bombers hit back at the German capital, Berlin.

Adolf Hitler, the German Führer, was convulsed with rage at Churchill's audacity. In a savage fury, he ordered Goering to smash London. He craved revenge. He meant Britain to pay dearly for the R.A.F. raids on Berlin.

On the 7th September, the blitz on London began, when wave after wave of German bombers droned over east London. Air raid sirens wailed their warning and Londoners hurried into cellars and air-raid shelters. As the sirens died away, the ear-piercing whine of falling bombs filled the air, followed by the muffled *crump* as they struck the slum houses and warehouses along the waterfront. Fire barges closed in on the blazing warehouses but the battle was a hopeless one. Flames swept through dockland engulfing all that lay in their path. And still the bombers came. For twelve hours the bombs continued to fall, wreaking havoc on the ground. In the air, the R.A.F. fought a heroic battle, shooting down 40 enemy aircraft for the loss of 22 of their own fighters.

The death toll on the ground was terrible. Four hundred men, women and children perished in that fearful attack. But if Hitler had hoped to break the Londoners' morale with his terror raids, he had greatly misjudged these Cockneys. The aerial bombardment bound the people together as never before. They emerged from their shelters and shattered houses resolved that they would not knuckle under, no matter what Hitler threw at them. Their cool courage and dogged determination in the face of adversity soon won them the admiration of the world and stood as an inspiration to others to fight on, no matter what the odds.

The Luftwaffe relentlessly continued its raids on London day after day, mercilessly pounding the Metropolis. The battle continued, but slowly the R.A.F. was tilting the balance in its favour. Although there were heavy losses on both sides, the score was about equal.

Sunday, 15th September, was the decisive day of the battle. It has been described as the greatest day in the history of the Royal Air Force. For Britain the outcome of the whole war depended upon the Spitfire and Hurricane pilots who were to fly that day.

The first hint of the impending attack came when the tiny blips began to appear on the British radar screens. The Germans were coming in their hundreds. Fighter Command, determined to smash the Luftwaffe once and for all, put every aircraft it could muster into the air. The resulting battle was an epic of aerial warfare. A thousand German aircraft attacked London, Bristol, Southampton, Liverpool and Manchester, closing in from all sides and clouding the skies like a plague of locusts. R.A.F. operations rooms buzzed with activity as more and more bombers crossed the coast.

The words of Squadron Leader Semple, an R.A.F. pilot of No. 504 squadron who was among those who fought that day, describe what it was like in the heat of that battle:

'At lunchtime on Sunday my squadron was somewhere south of the Thames Estuary behind several other squadrons of Hurricanes and Spitfires. The German bombers were three or four miles away when we first spotted them. We were at 17,000 feet and they were at about 19,000 feet. Their fighter escort was scattered around. The bombers were coming in towards London from the south-east and at first we could not tell how many there were. We opened our throttles and started to climb up towards them, aiming for a point well ahead where we expected to contact them at their own height.

'As we converged on them, I saw there were about twenty of them and it looked as though it was going to be a nice "party", for the other squadron of Hurricanes and Spitfires also turned to join in.

'By the time we reached a position near the bombers we were over central London. We had gained a little height on them too, so when I gave the order to attack we were able to dive on them from their right.

'Each of us selected his own target. Our first attack broke them up nicely. The Dornier I attacked with a burst lasting several seconds began to turn to the left, away from his friends. I gave him five seconds and he went away with white smoke streaming behind him.

'As I broke away and started to make a steep climbing turn, I looked over the side. I recognised the river immediately below and through a hole in the clouds I saw the bends in the river and the bridges and idly wondered where I was. I didn't recognise it immediately and then I saw Kennington Oval and I thought to myself: "That is where they play cricket." It's queer how, in the middle of battle, one can see something on the ground and think of something entirely different from the immediate job in hand. I remember I had a flashing thought – a sort of mental picture – a big man with a beard, but at that moment I did not think of the name W.G. Grace. It was just a swift, passing thought as I climbed back to the fight.

'I found myself very soon below another Dornier which had white smoke coming from it. It was being attacked by two Hurricanes and a Spitfire and it was still travelling north and turning slightly to the right. As I could not see anything else to attack at that moment, I went to join in. I climbed up above him and did a diving attack on him. Coming in to attack I noticed what appeared to be a red light in the rear-gunner's cockpit but when I got closer I realised I was looking right through the gunner's cockpit into the pilot and observer's cockpit beyond. The red light was fire.

'I gave it a quick burst and as I passed him on the right, I looked in through the big glass nose of the Dornier. It was like a furnace inside. He began to go down and we watched.

In a few seconds the tail came off and the bomber did a forward somersault and then went into a spin. After he had done two turns in his spin, his wings broke off outboard of the engines, so all that was left as the blazing aircraft fell was half a fuselage and the wing roots with engines on the end of them. This dived straight down, just past the edge of a cloud, and then the cloud got in the way and I could see no more of him.

'The battle was over by then. I couldn't see anything else to shoot at so I flew home. Our squadron's score was five certainties – including one by a sergeant pilot who landed by parachute in a Chelsea garden.

'An hour later we were in the air again, meeting more bombers and fighters coming in. We got three more – our squadron I mean. I started to chase one Dornier which was flying through the tops of the clouds....I attacked him four times altogether when he first appeared through the cloud – you know how clouds go up and down like foam on water – I fired at him from the left, swung over to the right, turned in towards another hollow in the cloud where I expected him to re-appear and fired at him again. After my fourth attack he dived down headlong into a clump of trees in front of a house and I saw one or two cars parked in the gravel drive in front. I wondered whether there was anyone in the doorway watching the crash.

'Then I climbed up again to look for more trouble and found it in the shape of a Heinkel 111 which was being attacked by three Hurricanes and a couple of Spitfires. I had a few cracks at the thing before it made a perfect landing on an R.A.F. aerodrome. The Heinkel's undercarriage collapsed and the pilot pulled up after skidding fifty yards in a cloud of dust. I saw a tall man get out of the right-hand side of the aircraft and when I turned back he was helping a small man across the aerodrome towards a hangar.'

That was a first hand account of one man's battles. That sort of action was repeated many times that Sunday. The skies, blackened by the waves of droning bombers and the great patterns of smoke over London, resounded to the chatter of machine-guns and cannon fire. Never had the German bomber and fighter crews faced such opposition. At the end of the day, the burning wrecks of 56 German aircraft were scattered across the countryside in southern England.

The R.A.F. had taken a terrible toll of the enemy with the loss of only 26 of their own aircraft.

Hitler flew into one of his classic tantrums when he heard of Goering's utter failure to defeat the R.A.F. The battle continued but now Hitler knew that his dream of invading Britain was over. A handful of R.A.F. pilots had dealt a crushing blow to the Luftwaffe, one from which it was never fully to recover.

The staggering truth is that, thanks to the supply efforts of men like Lord Beaverbrook, and to the spirit and strength of the organisation built up by its commander Air Chief Marshal, Sir Hugh Dowding, R.A.F. Fighter Command emerged from the battle stronger than it had been when the terrible conflict began.

When the Battle of Britain officially ended on 31st October, the Royal Air Force had, in less than four months, destroyed 1,733 German aircraft with the loss of 915 of their own. In that grim conflict, 375 British pilots lost their lives. But for the selfless courage of these young R.A.F. pilots the Second World War might have had a terrifying outcome for the British people.

12
The Legless Ace

Douglas Bader, a brilliant young R.A.F. pilot was one of the star turns at the Hendon Air Display, an annual event where the crack British pilots showed their skills to an excited public. His particular forte was formation aerobatic flying and time and again he gave dazzling displays of his skill as a pilot to an awe-struck audience. But now he was about to give a special performance for a group of young fellow R.A.F. officers who had dared him to put the Bristol Bulldog through its paces at low-level. At first Bader had declined to take up the dare because he had had several warnings from his senior officers about low-level flying. There were very strict rules about low-level aerobatics in the R.A.F. and Bader had already bent those rules once too often. He had had his final warning and had been told in no uncertain terms that any repetition would result in serious disciplinary measures being taken against him. Bader loved the R.A.F. and flying so he took the hint and was determined not to jeopardize a promising career.

However a few of his fellow officers had accused him of being chicken and to a man like Bader that was the ultimate challenge. He was boiling with rage.

'I'll show them,' he thought as he strapped himself in and quickly went through the pre-flight checks.

Burning with the determination to give them a display they would remember, Bader started the Bulldog's engine and the aircraft rolled forward over the grass. Then with the engine roaring at full throttle, the biplane lifted into the air.

The Bulldog gained the necessary height and wheeled round to begin its display. Bader plunged it earthwards then levelled off, flying only a few feet above the grass runway towards where the group of pilots stood. As the Bulldog shot across the grass Bader began a roll, holding the wing-tip off the ground as the wings became vertical. But just at the critical point, the Bulldog slipped slightly towards the ground and its wing-tip touched. Instantly the aircraft cartwheeled into the ground with a sickening crunch and crumbled into a tangled wreck like a collapsing pack of cards.

Horror-struck onlookers dashed to the tangled wreckage and found Bader trapped in the cockpit with his legs pinned in amongst its twisted metal. By some miracle he was still alive but only semi-conscious and willing hands feverishly tore away the wreckage to free him. Bader was only half aware of what was happening.

An ambulance screeched to a halt and Bader was rushed to hospital. The doctors examined him closely but soon formed the opinion that it was only a matter of time before he would be dead. His right leg had to be amputated just above the knee but somehow Bader still hung on to life though at one point his heart actually stopped beating for a time. Then to make matters worse, his left leg became infected and the surgeon had no choice but to amputate it also, just below the knee.

For days Bader lay desperately ill in hospital, unaware that he had lost both his legs. Mercifully when he did eventually discover the truth, he was under heavy sedation and was able to accept the catastrophe gradually. The pain that he suffered over the months that followed must have been appalling. All that remained of his legs were two stumps which ached continually. Lesser men would certainly have given way to the pain and died but Bader was a fighter. Since childhood he had been stubborn, determined and resourceful, but above all he was a battler who just would not give in. Without this inborn fighting spirit, he would never have survived those long months. Survival alone, however, was not enough for Bader. He wasn't going to let the loss of two legs interfere with his plans. He was a born flier and come what might, he was going to fly again....with or without legs!

To understand what went to make up a man of such courage, it is necessary to look back at his childhood because it was during those formative years that his streak of stubborn determination became ingrained in him.

Douglas Bader was born in St. John's Wood, London, on the 21st February, 1910, and began his education at Temple Grove Preparatory School in Eastbourne where, at the tender age of seven, he showed his fighting prowess by knocking out a classmate with one deft punch. Douglas instantly became a highly-respected member of the school.

In those days he was like a human dynamo with inexhaustible energy. He lived for games and threw himself into the school sports with almost wild fanaticism.

He excelled at every game he chose to play and even in his very young days he showed the sparks of courage that were to make him a demon in the air many years later. Battered and bruised in a tough rugger game, he would play on with even greater resolve refusing to submit to pain. With his natural sense of leadership and authority, even the older boys at school looked to him to show the way.

Douglas loved a challenge and never refused a dare – usually to his cost. There was an old tradition at Temple Grove that every boy should carve his name on his desk. Douglas regarded this as tame stuff and he pondered on how he could make an even more spectacular mark. Then one day he was passing the headmaster's greenhouse when he saw a great, fat vegetable lying snugly under glass – the Head's prize marrow. The temptation was just too great to resist. He drew his penknife from his pocket and carved the initials in the precious vegetable.

Even at home, young Bader had to find an outlet for his pent-up energy. He and his brother, Derek, spent their time poaching on the local farm land. Douglas was a crack-shot with an airgun and after a day's hunting usually came home with a full bag. But his skill with the air rifle was not always reserved for shooting game. Occasionally he found more tempting targets, like the lady who decided to take a mid-day bath. Douglas spotted her through a half-opened window. He just couldn't resist it. His finger squeezed the trigger, the window shattered and the lady leapt into the air with a scream.

Douglas's zest for life was untamed and as every day dawned, so he looked for another adventure to begin. Then one day he met an R.A.F. flight lieutenant called Cyril Burge, who had flown in the First World War. Douglas sat enthralled as the pilot told him of his exploits. The young boy's imagination was fired by the tales of daring. Burge was quick to see the boy's interest and invited him over to the R.A.F. College at Cranwell for a week's holiday. The highlight of the visit came when Burge led Douglas to an Avro biplane and allowed him to sit in the cockpit. Burge's stories came flooding back into the boy's mind and Douglas imagined himself wheeling through the air, duelling with the German aces.

Every day of that week spent watching the aircraft roaring off the grass airstrip, he longed to climb into one of these planes and experience the thrill of flight for himself. It was, therefore, with a heavy heart that he left Cranwell at the end of the week's stay. But by then he was resolved that one day he would return to Cranwell — as a pilot cadet.

Back at school, rugby, soccer, cricket and boxing filled his spare time. He excelled at all of them. In the boxing ring he had twenty fights and won nineteen of them by knockouts. Then came a near disaster; he caught rheumatic fever and for four weeks was close to death. He survived but it looked as if his sporting activities would have to be curtailed. However, Douglas had other ideas. With hard training he was soon back to his old form.

As the time grew nearer for him to leave school, he had to turn his thoughts to his future. He didn't take long to decide on the career he wanted to follow and he applied for entry to Cranwell.

Unlike today, when all entrants for Cranwell are selected according to ability and not social background, Bader was faced with a problem. Most cadets had to pay for entry to the college and Bader could not afford it. There was, however, just one chance. He could sit the examinations for one of the six prize scholarships granted annually by the college and if he passed, enter free. But the competition he would be up against was very strong. Hundreds of boys were entering for the scholarships.

Douglas had never been very enthusiastic about the academic side of his education and he realised that, if he were to stand any chance of a scholarship, he would have to work — and work really hard. He threw himself into studying with the same vigour he put into sport and after burning much midnight oil sat the examinations and faced the selection board. He felt fairly confident that he had done reasonably well but as the days passed he could not help remembering how many other boys were trying for a place.

Some weeks later, a letter arrived for him from the Air Ministry. He learned that he had come fifth in the exams and had won a scholarship. His hard work had paid off. Now he could hardly wait to pack his things and get to Cranwell.

One of Douglas's housemasters who had given him extra tuition for his exams presented him with a motorbike by way of congratulating him on his success. One day in September, he clambered on to his bike, kicked the foot starter, opened the throttle and roared off to Cranwell.

As his bike dashed along the road near the airfield he spotted an aircraft taking off. Craning his neck, he watched the plane zoom over his head. Intent on the aircraft, he forgot the road and careered off it, plunging into the bank. He shot through the air and landed in a heap on the ground, bruised and battered. It was a rather tattered cadet who presented himself at Cranwell. An irate warrant officer with a booming voice took one look at Bader and exploded in a fury. Already Douglas Bader had made a name for himself.

There followed the usual medical examinations, marathon form-filling, kitting-out sessions and endless hours of square-bashing (foot drill). He began to wonder when he would get into the air and begin the serious business of flying, but at last the day came. Wearing a brand new flying suit, helmet and goggles he dropped into the rear seat of an Avro 504 biplane and strapped himself in. His instructor, sitting in the front cockpit, opened the throttle, the flimsy biplane wobbled over the grass and lifted into the air. For the first time in his life, Douglas Bader was airborne. This, he knew with absolute certainty, was the life for him.

That very afternoon his flying training began in earnest and he was allowed to take control of the Avro for the first time. Almost immediately it was clear to his instructor that Bader was a 'natural' pilot. He had just the right 'touch' and flew the aircraft as if it were part of him. In a remarkably short time he was flying solo. Within a few more weeks he had gained his 'wings'.

With the vigorous Cranwell training over, Pilot Officer Bader was posted to his first squadron – number 23, where he was to fly Gloster Gamecock fighters.

Bader and the Gamecock made a superb pair. In fact he handled the plane so well that he was selected to join the famous R.A.F. aerobatics team to fly at the Hendon Air Pageant. The crowds gazed in awe at his superb flying and he soon made a name for himself. His special love was aerobatics – especially at low-level, where the swift rush of the ground past his cockpit lent flying that added touch of excitement. Inevitably Bader ended up 'on the carpet' a number of times for his 'dangerous flying', but in spite of this his future as a pilot seemed secure. Then came the fateful day in December 1931 when he crashed, losing both his legs....

The future for a pilot with no legs seemed non-existent to everyone else. At best, they thought, some sort of office job might be found for him. Even Bader wondered whether or not he would ever fly again. After ten months in hospital he was fitted with two artificial 'tin' legs. To begin with, wearing the legs was agonisingly painful because the limbs chaffed the tender skin on the stumps of his own legs. Determined that he would walk again, he persevered with the new limbs and to everybody's astonishment won the battle. Not only could he walk again but he could walk without the aid of sticks – something no one had ever previously managed to do.

Now his one thought was to get back into the air and prove that, once airborne, he could be as good as any other pilot with two 'real' legs. Apart from his disability he was superbly fit and he passed a medical examination with flying colours. Then a fellow pilot took him up for a flight and Douglas demonstrated beyond doubt that he had lost none of his old mastery. In spite of this, however, the R.A.F. declined to let him return to flying duties. Bader was stunned by the decision. He protested, but without success. Given a desk job, he found it unbearable to be so close to aeroplanes and yet not fly. At last, reluctantly, he resigned his commission and left the life he loved so much. He was bitterly downhearted.

Then Bader took a job in an office. It seemed that he would have to resign himself to what he felt to be a dull and uninteresting existence.

But when in 1939 Britain went to war once more, trained pilots were scarce. The day after war was declared, Bader got to work, writing letters and telephoning old friends in the R.A.F. Surely they would take him now, he thought.

More medical examinations followed and then a flying test in a Harvard trainer, the first monoplane he had ever flown. Although it had been seven years since he had last handled an aircraft on his own his natural flying skill came flooding back. He easily passed the test.

Soon Bader was back in the R.A.F. once more and posted to an operational squadron. It was there that he first flew a Spitfire fighter and he took to it like a bird to the air. This great new fighter with its superb lines and amazing manoeuvrability was a joy to fly.

But Bader wanted action. The days drew painfully on and still there was no sign of the enemy. His time was taken up with practice flights and convoy patrols over the English Channel.

Then the German army struck west into France and at last Bader thought he would have a chance to get into battle. But his hopes received a bitter blow. His squadron was posted north to Grimsby — away from the fighting.

As the furious battle raged in France Bader had to be content with waiting day after day in readiness. The news he heard of the British and German fighter clashes only made him even more impatient. Then came the epic rescue of the British forces at Dunkirk and at last, Bader's chance for action.

His squadron was thrown across the Channel to where the broken remnants of the Allied army lay. As Bader roared above the straggling lines of men wading out to the waiting craft, four Messerschmitt Bf 109 fighters pounced on the squadron. Bullets cut through the air towards the Spitfires as Bader and the others broke formation to face the enemy. Bader's thumb hovered over the firing button on his control column, poised for the kill. In a flash, a Bf 109 filled his sight and Bader's thumb jabbed the button. The Spitfire shuddered as the eight machine-guns in the wings burst into life. The German fighter rocked crazily as the bullets thudded home, riddling the fuselage with holes. Instantly flames shot out of the German fighter and it plunged towards the ground. Bader had made his first kill, but he was to wait a long time before he faced the enemy again.

By the time the Dunkirk evacuation was over, Bader held the rank of flight lieutenant and was in command of a flight of Spitfires. He had shown all the qualities of leadership, courage and skill which make a good commander and his superiors were quick to realise that he would go far. Fired with a determination to drive the Luftwaffe from the skies once and for all, he offered the kind of leadership the R.A.F. was looking for. In due course he was promoted to squadron leader and given command of his own squadron – number 242. At last he could use the tactics he had been planning so carefully.

Bader arrived at his new base to take command of the squadron only to find a bunch of battle-weary young pilots whose morale was at rock-bottom. They had suffered the humiliation of retreat in France and now, with their spirits for the fight almost completely eroded they had been given a commanding officer with tin legs! Bader could quickly sense the discontent and he had a pretty good idea why it existed. More than any other new commander he had to show them that he was as good as the next man....and even better.

Without hesitation, Bader stomped out of the crew room and over to a Hurricane parked nearby. Hoisting himself into the cockpit he roared off across the grass runway and into the air. There followed a stunning display of aerobatics. On the ground 242 Squadron's pilots watched open-mouthed as Bader hurled the Hurricane around the sky, rolling, looping, diving, spinning, climbing and screeching across the airfield a scant few feet above the grass. After half an hour of breath-taking aerobatics, he landed. From that moment on there was never any doubt in his pilots' minds that they had got as their leader the cream of the R.A.F's fighter pilots.

Bader was amazed to learn that, although he had a squadron of brand new Hurricanes, they had no spares because there was a mountain of form-filling to be done before he could get even a spanner. This infuriated Bader, and when things did that no one was likely to be left in much doubt about his feelings. There were a number of red faces when Bader went straight to the Commander-in-Chief Fighter Command and let him know in no uncertain terms why his squadron could not operate. Two days later the spares came rolling in. 242 Squadron was at last operational and ready for battle.

Bader's brilliant leadership and uncanny ability to get a man to do just what he wanted enabled him to mould his squadron into a highly-successful fighting team. He had his own ideas about how aerial battles should be fought. He believed, like Albert Ball before him, in 'scaring the pants' off the German bomber pilots by diving out of the sun headlong into the attack, breaking up the enemy formation and throwing it into confusion then launching attacks on its demoralised pilots from all sides. In the Battle of Britain that followed, Bader's tactics were devastatingly effective. German bombers and fighters tumbled from the sky under his guns. His own personal score rose rapidly and the squadron's victories soared under his leadership. In fact his tactics were so successful that he was called to the Air Ministry to advise on the question.

The pilots of 242 Squadron would now follow Bader into battle no matter what the odds: they had absolute faith in him.

Bader had more than one close shave in the heat of battle but miraculously he survived. He was awarded the D.S.O. and the D.F.C. for his leadership and courage. His exploits were legendary. When the Battle of Britain ended, his squadron went on the offensive, sweeping over France and shooting up any German target they could find.

But the Commander-in-Chief had realised that if Bader could work wonders with one squadron he could do even better with three. He was promoted to the rank of wing commander and given command of three squadrons of Spitfires. Although he was delighted, he left 242 Squadron and his many friends there with real regret.

Still, however, his energy seemed limitless. Even with two tin legs he was almost always the first man to his aircraft when his squadrons were scrambled into action. Yelling words of encouragement to his pilots over the intercom, he led his Spitfires into battle, tearing the heart out of the Luftwaffe. His unshakable confidence led many people to believe that he was unbeatable in the air. But alas, the day of reckoning had to come....

On that fateful day, Bader led his wing over the Channel to France, hunting for German fighters. It was not long before they found them and he launched an attack, racing in with guns blazing. A Messerschmitt went plummeting earthwards in flames, but as his victim screamed down, Bader's Spitfire lurched suddenly. Instantly, it began to topple towards the ground, half its fuselage missing. What had happened no one can be sure. Bader believes that a German fighter must have collided with his Spitfire. At any rate it was obvious then that he must get out – and fast.

Grabbing the cockpit canopy release he pulled and the canopy disappeared. Automatically his hands searched for the seat harness release and he freed himself. Then, hauling himself upwards into the rushing slipstream, he found that he was caught fast – by the leg. His right leg was jammed in the cockpit and the Spitfire was losing height at a terrifying rate. Pulling with all his might he managed to make the tin leg part company with his stump and fell away from the cockpit. Seconds later he was floating gently earthwards beneath his billowing parachute.

Below lay German-occupied France – and captivity. Taken prisoner as soon as he landed, he was rushed off to hospital where a doctor stared in amazed disbelief at this pilot without legs.

But if the Germans imagined that they had Bader 'in the bag' they were deceiving themselves. There was only one thought in his mind and that was escape. Luckily his damaged artificial leg was retrieved from the wreckage of his Spitfire and repaired. Though they could hardly be expected to realise it then, the Germans made a grave mistake in giving him back the use of his legs.

Immediately he began planning his escape. The ward door was guarded by a burly German trooper. That left him only one way out – through the window. But there was a drop of forty feet and he had no rope. Not to be defeated, he 'borrowed' several sheets from other patients and knotted them together. Then he hid his rope beneath a bed. He had solved one problem but there was another. It was one thing to escape from the hospital, but he could never hope to get back to England without the help of the French Resistance. However, his luck was in. A French nurse came to his aid and arranged that a man would wait outside the hospital every night on the stroke of midnight.

That night Bader slipped quietly out of bed fully clothed, tied the end of his improvised rope to a bed and threw the other end out of the window. Gingerly he slid down to the ground and crept towards the gate. Once outside he glanced around. There was a movement in the darkened doorway of a nearby house then a shape detached itself from the shadows.

Bader's heart beat faster. Was this the man — or was the game up already?

'Come quickly, monsieur!' the voice said. Bader heaved a sigh of relief and clutched the Frenchman's hand warmly. There was no time to waste: they had to move fast. Walking as quickly as he could with his stumps aching at every step, he scrambled through the darkness until he and his companion reached a cottage. The door creaked open and they slid inside to be greeted warmly by an old man and woman. Completely exhausted Bader slept soundly all night but at dawn he was awakened abruptly. The old man was shaking him.

'Monsieur! It is the Boche. The Germans have come and they are searching every house!'

The Frenchman shepherded Bader out of the back door to an outhouse and hid him under a pile of straw. As he lay beneath the straw he could hear the gutteral German voices. Then the back door of the cottage crashed open and jackboots crunched on the flagstones behind the house. Suddenly the door of the outhouse was thrown open and Bader heard the click as bayonets were fixed. In a flash a glinting blade was driven into the floor only inches from his arm. He had no choice but to give himself up. Back in hospital once more his legs were removed and without them he was helpless. The following day he was taken by train to a prisoner-of-war camp in Germany.

In the meantime, the Germans made contact with the R.A.F. through the Red Cross and a new right leg for Bader was parachuted during a bombing raid.

On his tin legs, Bader never gave up trying to escape and frustrated camp commandants kept moving him from one camp to another. Furious at being a prisoner he would not give the Germans a moment's peace. Treating them with complete contempt, he never missed a chance of making his captors look fools in front of their other prisoners. But the Cermans had a top security prison for 'special' prisoners who made habitual escape attempts. In due course Bader was sent to the notorious Colditz Castle.

The ancient fortress of Colditz dominated the land around it. With walls several feet thick encircled by a deep moat, the castle made escape almost impossible. Hand-picked guards kept an ever-watchful eye on Bader but despite the thought that he could never escape from Colditz, he did not for a moment relax his constant baiting of the Germans.

By then the Allied Forces were sweeping across Europe, pushing the German army back until one day a spearhead American force reached Colditz. Bader was free and a few days later was flown home.

Not long after his return to England, the war in Europe ended. Bader's greatest regret was that he could not have a last crack at the enemy. Before finally leaving the R.A.F. just after the war, he was promoted to the rank of Group Captain and given command of a whole fighter sector. But now the fight was over the real incentive was gone and Bader hung up his gloves.

Group Captain Douglas Bader, D.S.O. and Bar, D.F.C. and Bar, Légion d'Honneur, Croix de Guerre, was credited officially with shooting down twenty-three enemy aircraft, although the true total was probably nearer thirty. Bader fought two battles in that war, one against a determined and often ruthless enemy and the other against almost unbearable pain. His refusal to give in even in the face of tragedy has since then given fresh hope to countless thousands of disabled people throughout the world. Today he still works tirelessly in the cause of the handicapped and the unfortunate.

Douglas Bader was a brave and brilliant leader of men; a superb tactician, probably one of the finest pilots in the R.A.F. during the Second World War, and above all a man of unrivalled courage and limitless determination.

13
The Dam Buster Raid

Had it not been for the inventive genius and unflinching determination of one man, the most spectacular bomber raid of the Second World War would not have taken place. His name was Barnes Wallis and he was then – as he still is now – one of the most brilliant aircraft designers in the world.

It was Wallis who, between the two World Wars, designed Britain's most successful airship, the R.100, and it was he who gave the Royal Air Force the famous twin-engined Wellington bomber which, for a time, was the mainstay of Bomber Command and played such a vital role in the early years of the Second World War.

Wallis was a quiet and reserved man whose gentle manners and soft voice hid a streak of relentless resolution. He had an insatiable appetite for work and a keen eye for detail. Every problem was a challenge and none was too great for him to tackle. He would work day and night without thought of sleep or rest, wrestling with a problem which had been posed until it was solved.

When Britain declared war on Germany, Wallis turned his thoughts in the direction of how he could best help his country. He was an expert on bomb design and explosives so his calculating scientific brain set to work, pondering on how he could devise a weapon which would deal a crushing blow to the enemy. In his own methodical way he approached the problem by breaking it down to its basic elements.

'What was the one thing above all others upon which the German war machine depended?' he asked himself.

To Wallis the answer was all too clear – electricity. It was electrical power which drove the machines which in turn manufactured the guns, aircraft parts, torpedoes, shells, ships and so on. The production of all the weapons of war depended almost entirely upon the uninterrupted flow of electricity to the factories of the Ruhr and other vital industrial areas of Germany. The huge turbines which generated the electricity were themselves driven by water, millions of tons of it, and that water was stored in lakes created and kept in existence by dams. These lakes were situated near the sprawling miles of factories in the Ruhr. There was only one way to cut the flow of power to the factories and Barnes Wallis was quick to see it – smash the dams.

Not only would factory production stop instantly, but if a dam could be breached, millions of tons of water would gush out, drowning vast areas of land. Roads and railways, which formed the lifeline along which supplies rolled to the German soldiers at the front, would be flooded. The vital links between factory and front would be severed. Wallis had his targets, but the biggest problem of all now faced him – how to design a bomb which would be capable of blasting a hole in a great wall of solid concrete. None of the bombs in the R.A.F's arsenal at that time would even have scratched the surface of a dam wall, let alone have cracked it – and none could have been dropped accurately enough to hit such a narrow target.

For many weeks Wallis burned the midnight oil ferreting through books, technical magazines and scientific papers, searching for the germ of an idea which would lead him to a solution of the problem. Then he discovered it – an article on 'shock' waves written in a technical magazine. If he could not *blast* a breach in the dam, he could *shake* it down. Then Wallis immersed himself in figures, working out how much explosive would be required to breach one of the three major dams in the Ruhr — the Eder, Möhne and the Sorpe.

However, the greatest problem of all still faced Wallis. To be effective, the bomb had to explode on the bed of the reservoir, hard up against the dam wall. He knew only too well that the R.A.F. did not have a bomb-sight capable of such precise accuracy and the whole success of the idea depended entirely upon the bomb being dropped in exactly the right place. The slightest error would mean failure. Wallis racked his brain for the answer. Then it came. Something in his mind clicked. He remembered a game he used to play as a boy, throwing stones out to sea and watching them skip across the surface. He recalled the stones slowing as they skipped then stopping to float gently to the bottom of the sea.

'This could be it,' he thought. 'It might just work.'

Wallis lost no time in building a water tank in his garden and testing his idea. He tried a whole variety of shapes of 'bomb' until he finally found the shape which suited his purpose. Using a catapult-like device he fired his 'bomb', shaped rather like an oil drum, across the water until it gently hit the end of the tank to float to the bottom and come to rest against the wall of the tank in exactly the right position.

A whole series of tests still had to be carried out but first he had to get the 'green light' from the Service Chiefs. He had to convince them that his plan would work. But he met with a cool reception. Try as he might, no one was prepared to take a chance. Wallis was downhearted but determined not to give up.

To prove his theory, he managed to get permission to test his bomb on an old dam in the Welsh hills. He lowered the bomb into position on the lake bed against the dam wall then retreated to a safe distance and fired it. Instantly the calm water erupted like a bubbling cauldron near the wall. When the turmoil of water had subsided there was a gaping hole in the dam wall. The test was a complete success. Now surely, Wallis felt, the Service Chiefs must be convinced. But no, once more he received the same polite, but cool, refusal to take up the idea.

Back he went to work. This time he set about building a

dummy bomb, an exact copy of what the real one would be like. Armed with a camera and with the bomb loaded in the bomb-bay of a converted Wellington bomber, he took off to try it out at sea. On the first run the bomb shattered when it hit the water. Another bomb was duly built with a strengthened outer casing and on the second trial run the bomb worked perfectly.

Before he had a chance to present his findings, he received a telephone call telling him to stop work on the bomb immediately.

The story of Barnes Wallis and his bouncing bomb might well have ended there had it not been for a meeting he had with Air Marshal Sir Arthur 'Bomber' Harris, Chief of R.A.F. Bomber Command. The 'Bomber' was a man of few words and lots of action. Wallis explained his plan to him and showed him films he had shot of his bomb. Harris was impressed and quick to see the potential of this weapon. In a few days Wallis got the 'green light' to go ahead. That was in February, 1943, three years after he had first had the idea.

It was to be a race against time. The attack on the dams had to be made in May when the lakes were brim full of water. In that short space of time the bomb had to be manufactured in quantity and a special squadron formed to carry out this dangerous and vital mission.

Wallis worked day and night on the bomb while 'The Bomber' picked the man who was to lead the special Lancaster squadron. He chose a young Wing Commander who had already distinguished himself in raids on Germany. The young pilot (he was just twenty-five) had already flown on more than one hundred and seventy missions over enemy territory and in doing so earned the D.S.O. and D.F.C. He was Guy Gibson, a man to whom courage was second nature and a dynamo of energy. Faced with what seemed like an impossible task, he had only a few weeks to pick and train a crack bomber squadron.

Gibson lost no time in selecting his crews. He chose veterans – men who had already proved themselves in battle – men with strong nerves who would not crack under stress. All those he picked already knew the dangers and had learned to live with them as well as any man could.

Such complete secrecy was observed that even Gibson himself was not told what his target was to be or indeed in which country it was located. The slightest whisper of an intended raid would have the Germans racing to prepare strong defences around their dams and that was something the R.A.F. wanted to avoid at all cost. The dams were already defended by anti-aircraft guns mounted on towers at either end of the walls so they were, in any case, going to be tricky enough to hit without substantial losses of aircraft.

Avro Lancaster bombers had been specially chosen to carry out the raid. They were the finest bombers in service with the R.A.F. at the time, with wing spans of 102 feet and an overall length of 69 feet 6 inches. Powered by four 1390 h.p. Rolls Royce Merlin engines they could cruise at 210 m.p.h. They were heavily armed with eight .303 inch Browning machine guns and could carry up to 22,000 pounds of bombs. On normal bombing raids they carried a crew of seven.

As the days passed and the huge specially adapted Lancaster bombers began arriving at the airfield, Gibson was still in the dark about the target. All he knew was that, whatever it was, they were to attack it at low-level as he had been given orders to carry out intensive low flying training missions. Day after day, night after night his bombers roared at tree-top height through the valleys of Wales and Scotland and often the aircraft returned to base with great clumps of leaves stuck in their wings and fuselage.

While Gibson's squadron engaged in hazardous low-flying practice, Wallis was tackling the problem of how the Lancasters could deliver the bombs with pin-point precision. To be absolutely accurate, the bombs had to be dropped from a height of exactly sixty feet and at a precise distance from the dam wall. The altimeters, which indicate the height of an aircraft, were not sufficiently accurate to ensure that the bombs would be dropped from precisely 60 feet, so some other device had to be invented – and quickly. As often happens in science, the answers to difficult problems are found in remarkably simple ways. One of the backroom boys came up with the idea of using two searchlights installed in the belly of the aircraft. The searchlights would be pointing downwards and angled inwards and, when lit, the spots of light would be pre-set so that they would merge into one when the aircraft was flying at exactly 60 feet. On the approach to the target, one of the crew would give the pilot a running commentary on the position of the spots of light on the water so that he could either lift or drop the aircraft until the two spots merged into one. When tested, this amazingly simple device proved to be astonishingly accurate.

Yet another boffin solved the problem of dropping the bomb at the correct distance from the dam wall. He showed Gibson a triangular piece of wood which was to be held *horizontally*, with its apex towards the user. It had a peep-hole 'sight' fixed over its apex and a nail sticking up from each of its other two corners. The idea was that the bomb-aimer would peer through the peep-hole and line up the nails onto the two towers on the dam wall. When the nails were in line with both towers, then was the time to release the bomb. It seemed too simple to be true but when tested it was, like the searchlights, absolutely accurate. All seemed to be going well.

At last Gibson was briefed on the target but it was not until the day before the raid, on May 15th, that he revealed to his assembled crews what that target was. In the briefing room the crews sat in silence as Gibson told them of their mission. Weeks of uncertainty had led to wild speculation amongst them but now they knew the truth. This was to be the toughest raid Bomber Command had ever undertaken and each one of these airmen knew the risks involved. Their chances of survival were almost suicidally slim but not one of them would have backed out.

The following day, the specially converted Lancasters were loaded up with the huge bombs. Nineteen aircraft were to take part in the raid, split into three attacking formations. They were going to hit all three dams.

Gibson, with nine aircraft, was to attack the Möhne dam then go on to the Eder while a second formation of five aircraft was to attack the Sorpe. Five other Lancasters were to take off later to act as a back-up force if needed.

Throughout the day the tension mounted as the crews went methodically about the business of preparing for the raid. Nervous excitement was always at its peak just before take-off. At last the time came for the crews to clamber aboard the great four-engined aircraft parked by the runway and shortly after nine-o'clock the Lancasters took to the air....some of them for the last time.

As the bombers crept across the North Sea, Barnes Wallis

paced nervously up and down the operations room where he and 'Bomber' Harris, along with other high-ranking officers waited for reports from the raiders. Gibson had arranged to flash the codeword 'Nigger' to the operations room if the mission were a success. He had good reason to choose that word. Nigger was his dog and faithful companion. They had been inseparable and Gibson had taken him on many missions. But a few days before the big raid. Nigger had been killed by a car just outside the airfield.

The Lancasters thundered across the sea, flying only a few feet above the waves to avoid detection by German radar. One pilot flew so low that his Lanc scooped up hundreds of gallons of water. The impact of the water ripped the belly clean off the Lancaster and tore the bomb from its bay. Miraculously, the pilot managed to heave the aircraft free of the water and without its bomb had no choice but to turn back for home.

As Gibson's nine Lancasters slipped across the Dutch coast into enemy-held territory, disaster struck the other formation for the second time. As its lead aircraft drove inland suddenly the flak gunners on the ground got it pinpointed. Bullets and shrapnel lashed the Lanc, smashing through the fuselage and wrecking the radio and intercom. The pilot, Squadron Leader Munro, who was to have directed the attack on the Sorpe, knew he could never carry out his mission without radio. Cursing his luck, he turned for home.

That left only three Lancs in the Sorpe formation and one of those was trailing far behind because of a late take-off. The two that now skimmed over the Dutch countryside flew headlong into a concentration of anti-aircraft fire against which they stood no chance. Within minutes they were both blazing wrecks on the ground.

The attack had not yet begun and already there had been four casualties. As Gibson's formation raced towards the Rhine, almost touching telegraph wires and tree-tops, the sky became a blaze of light. The searchlights were probing. Tracer bullets whipped up from the ground and zipped past Gibson's Lanc.

'Get those lights!' Gibson yelled to his gunners.

Instantly the Lanc shook as the front and rear gunners swung their turrets and poured their fire at the sources of light. Searchlight crews dived for cover as a hail of fire raked their emplacements. Bullets smashed into the huge lights, extinguishing a number. The formation roared on, deeper into Germany but, unknown to Gibson at that time, one of his Lancs commanded by Flight Lieutenant Bill Astell had fallen victim to the heavy flak and crashed.

As the seconds ticked by the formation neared its target. Gibson's aircraft weaved through the hills until, suddenly, there it was, a huge artificial lake shimmering in the moonlight.

Gibson got his aircraft into attacking order but no sooner had he done so than the anti-aircraft guns on the dam opened up. The sky was soon laced with multi-coloured tracer trails as the German gunners fired wildly at the Lancs.

'I'm going in,' Gibson said coolly over the intercom and the Lancaster wheeled round and levelled off, thundering towards the lake. At 240 m.p.h., the huge aircraft ate up the ground then skimmed out over the lake. Ahead were the dam towers. On went the two searchlights underneath the aircraft and instantly the German gunners swung their guns onto the lone attacking aircraft. Hundreds of rounds of ammunition hurtled towards the bomber, but Gibson held her steady, concentrating on the voices heard through the intercom. Lying flat in the nose, the bomb-aimer peered down at the two spots of light thrown by the searchlights on the water.

'Up a bit, skipper!' the bomb-aimer urged. 'Down slightly – up – up – hold it – steady. *There!*' The two spots of light had become one.

His arms taut, Gibson held the aircraft right on sixty feet as it roared towards the dam wall. The bomber-aimer lined up the two nails of his crude distance calculator with one hand while the other was poised over the bomb release button.

'Bomb gone!' he yelled and the great black shape detached itself from the Lancaster and hit the surface of the water with a huge splash. The bomb skipped across the water as the Lanc roared over the dam wall where it was caught in the cross-fire from the German guns mounted on the towers. Gibson pushed the control column forward and dived into the valley out of range of the guns. Meanwhile the bomb slowed and slid down the inner wall of the dam, just as Wallis had predicted it would.

Gibson glanced round as he pulled the Lancaster up into a climb. Suddenly the water near the wall shot up into the sky as the bomb exploded. A huge cheer went up in the bomber. The water boiled like a furious cauldron, then gradually subsided. But the dam was still intact, so Gibson ordered the next aircraft to attack.

The second Lanc chased across the water but the German gunners found their mark. Its port wing burst into flames as its fuel tank caught fire. Crippled, the Lancaster shot over the dam wall, crashed and exploded. Horror-struck, Gibson ordered the next Lanc, flown by Squadron Leader 'Micky' Martin to start its attack. The Lancaster charged down the lake as Gibson roared across the dam, trying to draw the gunners' fire. Gibson's Lanc was a sitting duck for the gunners but they were wise to his trick and they had spotted Martin's Lanc so they concentrated on him. Unheeding, Martin thundered on and released his bomb. Seconds later there was an almighty explosion but *still* the wall held.

As the next aircraft attacked Gibson once more dashed across the lake drawing the enemy fire. Again the bomb exploded bang on target but the stout wall withstood the blast. The next aircraft in was Flight Lieutenant Maltby's. This time both Gibson and Martin flew alongside the attacking aircraft with guns blazing away at the towers. Down went Maltby's bomb and the three aircraft swept over the dam wall. A violent explosion sent the water shooting into the sky and Gibson craned his neck to see the wall.

'Holy mackerel!' someone yelled. 'It's gone! We've smashed it!'

The mighty wall cracked and thousands of tons of concrete tumbled into the valley, leaving a vast hole. One hundred and thirty million tons of water raced down the valley mercilessly sweeping aside all that lay in its path. Houses crumbled under the impact, bridges collapsed and in a few minutes the whole valley was a torrent of water. Nothing that lay in its path survived.

The Lancaster crews watched in stunned silence hardly able to believe their eyes. The destruction of the Möhne dam was complete. But their work was far from over. They left the scene of destruction and headed for their next target — the Eder.

Back in the operations room in England, a morse receiver suddenly chattered into life. One by one the letters they had all been waiting for were spelled out. N..I..G..G..E..R.

Cheers resounded through the ops room. Wallis was triumphant: his years of work had not been in vain. But there were still two more dams to be attacked.

The Eder was not protected by anti-aircraft guns but it presented another equally difficult problem. It was situated deep in a valley with high hills all around and diving in to attack it at night was very tricky. When the formation arrived, Squadron Leader Shannon's aircraft was the first to attempt an attack. He tried six runs on the dam but each time was dissatisfied with his positioning. So Gibson ordered the next aircraft in and down it went. The same thing happened. Twice the pilot tried but both times he failed. Only on the third run could he release his bomb with a chance of success. But then disaster struck. The bomb hit the dam wall just às the Lanc was crossing it. There was a tremendous explosion and the Lancaster, caught in the blast, crashed into the ground.

Shannon went in twice more and on the second run released his bomb. His patience paid off and the bomb exploded right on target, sending up a great plume of water. But the wall held. Only one aircraft was left with a bomb-load. Everything depended on this final bomb.

The last Lancaster delivered the bomb on its third run-in. Like Shannon's it found the mark. Gibson watched the wall with bated breath then gazed in awe as the vast expanse of concrete began to crumble. A great jet of water leapt out of the widening gap and thundered into the valley, ploughing through towns and villages.

'We've done what we came to do,' Gibson said over the intercom. 'Let's go home!'

The battered aircraft of his formation set course for England. As Gibson's Lancasters winged their way across Europe, dodging the flak, the sole surviving Lanc of the second formation was launching an attack on the Sorpe dam. Squadron Leader McCarthy, an American citizen who had joined the R.A.F., was piloting the lone Lancaster. But he was faced with an almost impossible task. The Sorpe was shrouded in mist and he had to fly 'blind' on to the target. He did, however, succeed in dropping his bomb but one bomb was not enough to shatter the solid ramparts. Disappointed he turned for home.

Group Headquarters ordered the back-up force of reserve

aircraft to attack the Sorpe but the odds against success were too great. They tried desperately to smash the dam but without success. Determined not to waste their bombs they diverted to another, smaller dam but heavy flak took its toll and more aircraft were lost. The attack had to be abandoned.

On the way back to England, Squadron Leader Young's Lancaster was hit by flak and ditched into the sea. Neither he nor his crew were ever seen again. Out of the force of nineteen aircraft which took part in the raids, only nine returned. Fifty-six airmen out of the one hundred and thirty who flew on the raid had perished. Barnes Wallis was overwhelmed. The size of the death toll came as an appalling shock to him and, while the survivors were celebrating their success, he sat alone, unable to believe that so many had died and wishing he had never invented his bomb.

The destruction caused by the raids was immense. Vast areas of land were engulfed in water. One hundred and thirty factories were wrecked, forty bridges were torn down, airfields were flooded and many Luftwaffe aircraft destroyed. Water poured into the maze of galleries in coalmines flooding them and making them useless. The lakes behind the Eder and Möhne dams lay almost empty. Over five hundred million tons of water had been let loose in seconds. If the final effect on German industry was not in the end quite as paralysing as had been hoped, it was still a staggering result.

At home the men of the special squadron which had been formed for the raid (Number 617) were national heroes. For his courage in leading the attacks Wing Commander Gibson was decorated with the Victoria Cross. In all, thirty-three men of the squadron were decorated for bravery.

Following the raid, a special squadron crest was designed for 617. It showed a breached dam with water pouring out of it and streaks of lightning above. The motto read: *Après nous, le déluge*. (After us, the flood.)

Gibson returned to fly with 617 squadron but was killed in action over Holland in 1944. The R.A.F. had lost one of its most courageous leaders.

Today Barnes Wallis continues to revolutionise flying with his brilliant designs. It was he who first thought of and designed the revolutionary swing-wing fighter. For more than fifty years this man's genius has provided the aircraft industry throughout the world with the stepping stones which have led it to supersonic flight. He was recently knighted for his contribution to aviation.

14
Commandos from the Sky

During the Second World War, the aeroplane was used in a large variety of ways as an offensive weapon, but principally in the role of fighter or bomber. It had, however, one other major role in the battle, that of transporting airborne troops – taking the soldiers to the war zones.

Thousands of paratroops were dropped from the sky or landed by glider behind the enemy lines, the most notable occasions being when three whole divisions of troops were dropped at Arnhem in 1944 and during the mighty invasion of Europe when thousands of troops were dropped far behind the invasion beaches to throw the defending Germans into confusion and attack their forces from the rear.

Few would have thought that in a highly-mechanised war the glider would have played a significant part, but it did and on one occasion it was the glider that saved the day for that famous, and ruthless, leader on the Axis side – Benito Mussolini.

The spring of 1943 saw for the Allies the victorious end of

the North African Campaign. The might of the German forces in the desert had been smashed and the territories in which so much bitter fighting had taken place, were now firmly in the grip of the Allied armies. With their victory in North Africa complete, the Allies now turned their attentions to Europe and launched a massive assault on Italy, first attacking the island of Sicily.

As a result of this invasion, Italy was thrown into confusion. More than a quarter of a million Axis troops had been lost fighting the Allies in North Africa and now the very security of the Italian mainland was threatened. In the eyes of many Italians, their bombastic, arrogant leader, Benito Mussolini, had failed his country miserably and it seemed that ignominious defeat was just around the corner. The Italians could ill-afford to suffer the same ignoble fate on home ground that they had done in North Africa. Basically a simple, life-loving people, they had been lured and tricked into a war few of them wanted and now their beloved homeland was about to become a battleground.

The Italians realised that something had to be done, very quickly, if they were to save Italy from total destruction. At a meeting of the Fascist Grand Council, Mussolini ('the Duce') was denounced and forced to resign. No sooner had he resigned from office than he was arrested on the orders of the King of Italy and made prisoner.

The news of Mussolini's arrest and imprisonment quickly reached the ears of Adolf Hitler, the German Führer, who flew into a blind fury and vowed that at all costs he would rescue his friend and ally from the clutches of the anti-war faction in Italy. Hitler knew only too well that the Italians would surrender without much of a fight when the eventual Allied invasion of the Italian mainland came but, if he could retrieve Mussolini from captivity, there still remained a slight hope that they might rally and put up a fight.

One day in mid-July 1943, shortly after the invasion of Sicily, six German officers of the S.S., the *élite* corps of the Nazi fighting forces, were summoned to Hitler's headquarters, hidden in a forest in East Prussia. The six men duly arrived at the lonely headquarters and were shown into a reception room where they awaited the arrival of their Führer. They were all tall men of superb physique. Each of them was a veteran fighter who had shown himself unswervingly loyal to the Nazi cause.

None of the six men had the slightest idea as to why he had been summoned, but no guess any of them made could have been as strange as the truth. Only one man knew what was in store for them – or at least for one of them – and he had not yet joined them.

At last the door opened and Hitler's aide marched into the room.

'*Achtung!*' he barked and the six men leapt to their feet.

A second later, Hitler himself entered the room, with bent back and pale, drawn face. He was dressed as he usually was, in a grey uniform open at the neck to reveal a white shirt and black tie. His only decoration was the black Iron Cross First Class which he wore on his left breast. He stopped before the assembled men and each of them clicked his heels and gave the Nazi salute.

Few Germans, save his closest advisers and the High Command, had the opportunity of seeing Hitler in the flesh in those troubled days, and he may even have seemed a disappointing figure to these young S.S. officers. The 'superman' who had once led them to victory over Europe no longer resembled the man they must have remembered. Here before them stood a broken man, obviously ill, with trembling hands and a heavily-lined face showing all the marks of strain.

One by one the assembled men were introduced to Hitler and asked to give an account of their war records. Hitler listened patiently to each man in turn then he addressed them *en masse* in a voice which must have surprised them for it was still strong and purposeful.

'Which of you know Italy?' he enquired of them.

There was a momentary pause then one of the officers stepped forward and spoke. He was Otto Skorzeny, a fifteen stone mountain of a man but in first rate condition.

'I have travelled through Italy twice, my Führer,' he said.

Hitler nodded, acknowledging Skorzeny's answer then asked him....

'And what is your opinion of Italy?'

The question Hitler had posed was a difficult one to answer truthfully. The bulk of the German forces who had fought alongside the Italians or knew of them in battle did not have a very high regard for their fighting spirit, yet

Skorzeny knew that Mussolini was Hitler's most trusted ally and he had to exercise caution in answering.

Skorzeny's predicament was further complicated by the fact that he was an Austrian and no love had been lost between Austria and Italy since the South Austrian Tyrol had been ceded to Italy in 1918. At length, in reply to Hitler's question, Skorzeny said to Hitler....

'I am an Austrian, my Führer...'

Hitler knew only too well what Skorzeny meant and asked for no further explanation. He paused thoughtfully for a moment, then he instructed all of the officers to leave with the exception of Skorzeny.

When at last the two men were alone Hitler looked at Skorzeny, weighing him up, then he took him into his confidence. Skorzeny, Hitler told him, had been picked for a mission of the greatest importance. The Führer's most trusted ally and friend, Mussolini, had been taken prisoner and must at all costs be rescued before he was handed over to the Allies. The task of finding the Duce and rescuing him from captivity was being given to Skorzeny. Speed was of the essence as the fate of the Duce hung in the balance.

As he spoke, Hitler was visibly moved. Skorzeny knew that, above all else, the rescue of his friend was the Führer's most earnest wish. How he was to perform this seemingly impossible task, he did not know, but somehow, he resolved, he would.

The two men talked at some length, then Hitler left the room secure in the knowledge that if anyone could rescue the Duce, it was Skorzeny.

The young S.S. officer, who was already head of a special German commando unit which he had led with distinction, lost no time in getting down to work. He immediately got in touch with his second in command in Berlin, telling him to stand by for instructions which would follow almost immediately and ordering him to pick fifty of his best men for a special mission. The only added qualification they would need was a working knowledge of Italian. Throughout the night his 'hot-line' to Berlin was kept busy as he issued further instructions to his second in command, concerning the large quantities of arms and ammunition and all the supplies and equipment he would require.

The mission given to Skorzeny was made doubly difficult

because neither he nor German intelligence had the remotest idea of where Mussolini was being held captive. Discovering this would be his first task, then he could make full plans for his rescue. But wherever the Duce's captors were holding him, it was already pretty obvious to Skorzeny that he would have to launch an airborne assault on the prison. This, he concluded, was the swiftest and surest means of surprising the Duce's captors and achieving success. Time was fast running out for the Italian dictator and Skorzeny knew that if he was to find Mussolini he must go to Italy and do it himself.

Skorzeny flew to Rome with General Student, of the Luftwaffe, under whose direct orders he would come. In spite of his being answerable to Student, he knew that he would have a completely free hand to carry out the operation. Once in Italy, he got down to work, vetting every piece of information that came to hand. The Italians had gone to great lengths to lay false trails, knowing that some attempt would probably be made to rescue the Duce. Nevertheless Skorzeny persevered. Rumours as to the Duce's whereabouts ran rife throughout Italy and he followed up every morsel of information that came his way but without success.

By the middle of August, he was a worried man. The Axis forces in Sicily had succumbed to the weight of the Allied invasion and an attack on Italy was now imminent. He must act soon.

Then his luck changed. Skorzeny got wind of someone important being held prisoner at Santa Maddelina in Sardinia. This, Skorzeny thought, might be the clue he had been searching for. Collecting Lieutenant Wagner, who spoke fluent Italian, he set off for the island.

Once in Sardinia, Skorzeny had to get positive proof that it was indeed Mussolini who was being held there. There would be little point in mounting a raid only to find that they had been on a wild goose chase. So he devised a plan to get that proof. He instructed Wagner to disguise himself as a German sailor and frequent the dockside taverns which Skorzeny knew were a hot-bed of information freely given by drunken sailors and locals alike.

Day and night, Wagner did a round of the dockside alehouses where he kept his ear to the ground in the hope that some tit-bit of information as to the Duce's whereabouts might come in his way. But alas not a whisper was heard. Then Skorzeny had another bright idea. He knew every Italian's liking for a bet and he told Wagner to return to the inns and, feigning drunkenness, proclaim in a loud voice that the Duce was dead and that he would bet good money that he was right.

This Wagner did and it was not long before the bait caught the fish in the shape of a local fruiterer, who swore that he knew Mussolini was alive – and furthermore could prove it. He even claimed that he had seen him with his own two eyes at the Villa Weber while he had been delivering fruit there.

But Wagner was not convinced. Playing the old man along, he said that he would only pay up on the bet if he saw the Duce himself. To Wagner's utter amazement, the old man said that he could even arrange that. The following day he took the German to a house next door to the Villa Weber where he had to deliver some fruit. He pointed to a man sitting on a balcony in the house next door. Wagner could hardly believe his eyes. It certainly looked like the Duce and he hurriedly paid the bet and made his way back to Skorzeny.

When he heard the news Skorzeny immediately set about devising a plan to raid the villa by using his own troops landed from a fast motor-boat near the villa, supported by other S.S. troops from Corsica. No sooner had he completed his plan when he got the shattering news that the bird had flown....the Duce had vanished from the villa. Once more Skorzeny had to begin playing the game of detective.

It was Skorzeny's own intelligence men who finally tracked down the missing Duce to a hotel situated high in the Abruzzi Mountains....one of the most inaccessible places in Italy.

Again he set about devising a plan of attack, but first he had to reconnoitre the target so he and his adjutant set off in a light plane for a flight over the hotel.

The little aircraft soared over the jagged peaks of the mountains until at last, Skorzeny caught sight of the hotel, perched 6000 feet above sea level in a remote spot. Clutching a camera, Skorzeny leant out of the aircraft and took photographs of the hotel and the surrounding area so that he could get the lie of the land before planning the raid. He also noticed that there was a field behind the hotel where a glider-borne force might be landed. Back at his base the pictures were quickly processed and he got down to studying them.

But even as he scrutinised them the war in Italy was taking a dramatic turn which made his job all the more urgent. Fighting had broken out between German and Italian forces around Rome, so if he was to succeed in his raid it would have to be attempted soon.

After considering every possible method, Skorzeny decided on a glider-borne attack. The gliders, towed to their slip-off points by powered aircraft would carry his assault troops who would use the well-tried shock tactics which had proved so successful in past campaigns. An element of surprise was of the utmost importance. They had to act swiftly, before the Italian guards had time to call up reinforcements.

Skorzeny discovered from his intelligence sources that the hotel was guarded by 250 crack Italian mountain troops who had orders to fight to the last man if the hotel was raided by German forces. His soldiers were likely to face formidable opposition from these troops who were renowned for their courage in battle.

The German commando leader had hurried consultations with Luftwaffe experts who assured him that it would be impossible to land more than a few gliders in the restricted space of the field behind the hotel. Furthermore, the air at that height would be thin and keeping the gliders' airspeed down for a landing without them stalling would be extremely difficult. But Skorzeny was not to be deterred. He had had his orders from the Führer himself and he was determined to carry them out.

The twelve gliders were duly assembled at the airfield, ready for the raid which was planned to take place at dawn on September 12th. The day before, however, the Allies launched a bomber attack on the airfield and the strip became pitted with craters. Nevertheless, it was decided that the raid must go ahead as planned.

On the same day, the Allies broadcast a message that Mussolini had been handed over to them and was now under armed guard in North Africa. For a while Skorzeny thought that the Allies had got in first but a few minutes with a map of the Mediterranean convinced him that no ship could have made the voyage to Africa in the time since the purported hand-over.

Skorzeny was, however, still worried about the weight of resistance he and his men might encounter when they attacked the hotel and he wondered how he could throw the Italians into confusion, if only for a few minutes, when his own force landed. After all, the Italians might be tempted to kill the Duce rather than let him fall into German hands. Perhaps, he thought, if he were to take along an Italian officer, the sight of an Italian uniform might just confuse his enemies for the vital few minutes it would take his own men to gain the upper hand. Never content with doing things by halves, Skorzeny enlisted the aid of an Italian general willing to come along on the raid.

Soon it was time for the take-off and with all the commandos on board their gliders, the two-aircraft pulled them into the air. All, that is except two which hit bomb craters on the runway and were smashed to pieces. Skorzeny, left with only ten gliders for the attack, hoped that there would be no more mishaps. But as the formation of gliders and tow-planes cruised over the mountains disaster struck again when the two leading gliders collided and plunged to earth. Now he was left with only eight gliders, a sadly depleted strike force.

At last the slip-off point came and the gliders were released from their tow-aircraft to sink down towards their landing area. Gradually the drone of the aircraft died away and the commandos huddled in the gliders seemed to be plunging into a void, the stillness broken only by the swish of the air rushing past them.

Now they were only minutes away from the beginning of the attack. Skorzeny glanced out of the glider window at the field his glider was heading for only to see to his horror that, far from being flat, it rose steeply and worse still was strewn with huge boulders. But there could be no turning back. To find another landing place, even if there was one to be found, would mean losing the element of surprise that was so vital to the success of the raid. So Skorzeny yelled to the pilot to crash land and a few seconds later the glider smashed into the ground. Rocks tore at the fuselage and the aircraft ground to a halt, a tangled wreck. Half dazed but still aware of his mission, Skorzeny stumbled out of the wreckage and dashed towards the hotel with several others hot on his heels. Ahead of him he could see an Italian sentry riveted to the spot where he stood, unable either to believe his eyes or to make up his mind what to do. Skorzeny could have shot him dead there and then but sensing the man's plight and knowing that he was incapable of action, he darted past him and into an open door nearby.

Once inside Skorzeny saw a wireless operator sitting at his set. Realizing that he must on no account be allowed to transmit, Skorzeny kicked the seat from under the man and smashed the radio with the butt of his gun. No one could raise the alarm now. With that done, the commando leader darted out of the hotel again and rounded a corner. As he did so, he could see other gliders landing in the field and breaking up on the boulders. Men were being tossed out of the wrecked machines as they slithered along the ground.

Once at the front of the hotel, Skorzeny glanced quickly at the windows, scanning them for signs of life. There, at one, was a face — pale, drawn, but unmistakable. It was Mussolini.

Like a man possessed, Skorzeny dashed in through the front door of the hotel only to find himself in a hallway packed with Italian troops. Launching himself in amongst them like a missile he carved a way through the sea of bodies. Then darting up a flight of stairs onto a landing he threw open the first door he came to. His luck held. Standing before him, ashen faced, was the man he had been hunting for so long, the Duce himself. But with him were two Italian officers....

At that moment Skorzeny was joined by another commando who waved his gun in the faces of the two officers and bundled them out of the room, slamming the door behind them. Bewildered, Mussolini could hardly speak. Skorzeny tried to explain his mission but just then the Italian commandant entered the room.

This, Skorzeny knew, was the decisive moment. So far not a shot had been fired, but if the Italian were to put up a fight, then the operation could easily turn into a blood-bath. Skorzeny decided to try a bold approach. He told the Italian that he had thirty seconds in which to surrender or die. The Italian hesitated for a moment then left the room, returning a minute later with a goblet of wine which he handed to

Skorzeny.

'To the victor!' the Italian said. There was to be no blood-bath.

With Mussolini securely in his hands, Skorzeny was now faced with the problem of how to get him out of the mountain eyrie. Taking him down the mountain would mean facing more Italian troops who might not be quite so willing to surrender. It was then that he saw a Fieseler Storch aircraft circling overhead. The Storch was a light aircraft which could land in a surprisingly small space. Skorzeny quickly ordered his men to clear the boulders away from the field and make a suitable landing place.

As soon as the aircraft had rolled to a halt, Mussolini was bundled aboard and Skorzeny followed him. The pilot pleaded with him not to come saying that with such a load the aircraft would never be able to get off the ground but Skorzeny was determined to try and the tiny aeroplane, with the engine revving its life out, trundled along the makeshift runway and just managed to claw its way into the air. After a slow and hair-raising flight, it touched down in Rome. Skorzeny's mission was complete. The Duce was safe....or so he thought.

When he heard of the success of Skorzeny's mission, Hitler immediately conferred Germany's highest honour upon him, the Knight's Cross. Indeed he was so delighted that he ordered one of Skorzeny's fellow officers to hand over *his* Knight's Cross to Skorzeny so that he might receive it without delay.

Otto Skorzeny had successfully carried out a courageous and daring operation which shook the Allies, but when one considers that on Mussolini's return to Italy he was murdered by his own people and left hanging from a lamppost, it is doubtful if the young commando did him much of a service.

15
Fire in the Sky

Throughout the Second World War aircrews in bombers and fighters alike faced many dangers but the one which these courageous men dreaded more than any other was fire. Few airmen who flew on missions over enemy territory did not at some time witness a blazing aircraft hurtling earthwards in a death dive. In a few seconds even a mighty bomber could be totally engulfed in searing flames with its crew unable to bale out. Countless hundreds of men perished in this way. But horrifying as it was to witness such sights, it was fire that drove many airmen on to almost unbelievable deeds of courage and bravery. Here are the stories of just a few of these staggering feats of valour....

The most miraculous escape of all from a blazing bomber during World War Two was enacted over Germany during a night raid on Berlin....

Sergeant Nicholas Alkemede peered out of the perspex dome of his cockpit into the dark night sky over the Reich. His aircraft, along with a huge formation of others, was nearing the target. He was the 'tail-end-charlie' (rear-gunner) in a Lancaster bomber and he knew that the action would come soon. Berlin was one of the most heavily defended cities in Germany, ringed with fighter bases and protected by hundreds of anti-aircraft guns. He knew only too well that when his formation was discovered by the enemy, the night-fighters would be dashing into the sky to intercept them before they reached the German capital.

Alkemede, sitting isolated in the tail of the aircraft, swung his turret to and fro and peered out into the inky darkness for any sign of the fighters that were sure to come when the alarm was raised. He felt remote and alone, cut off from the rest of the crew up front. His only link with the others was through the intercom which crackled into life only occasionally when the skipper gave orders to the crew.

The job of tail-end-charlie was perhaps the most dangerous of all in a bomber. He was totally exposed to enemy fighters which invariably launched their attacks on bombers from the rear, raking them with cannon and machine-gun fire. It was not at all uncommon for a bomber to return to base in England only to find that the rear-gunner had been killed or seriously wounded. The mortality rate amongst rear gunners was higher than amongst any other members of bomber crews. It was not a comforting thought for Alkemede as the huge Lancaster droned its way deeper into Germany towards the target.

From his cockpit, Alkemede got a panoramic view of the rest of the formation as it thundered through the sky. Soon they were over Berlin but by then the hornet's nest had been stirred and dozens of German night-fighters were darting into the sky to do battle with the invaders.

In a flash a German fighter swept in on Alkemede's Lanc with cannon blazing. Shells lashed into the Lancaster's fuselage then the perspex dome in front of Alkemede disintegrated as two shells smashed it to pieces. But by then Alkemede had a bead on the fighter and his machine-guns were chattering, pumping a hail of bullets at the fighter. Beads of sweat poured from the young gunner's brow and into his eyes but still he blasted away at the fighter. He could just see his tracer bullets whipping into the German aircraft then as it plunged past his turret, a great tongue of flame leapt from it.

'Got 'im!' he yelled triumphantly. But his moment of triumph was quickly cut short when he glanced round and saw that the fuselage behind him had been transformed into a blazing tunnel of fire, roaring like a furnace. For a moment he was too horror-stricken to move but quickly he collected his wits and struggled from his seat. His first thought was to get his hands on his parachute and he struggled from his seat and made a dive for the 'chute which was stowed only a few feet away in the fuselage. But to his horror he saw that the fire had got to it first. It was burnt to a cinder.

By then the bomber was dipping towards the ground and Alkemede realised that he was doomed. Either he would be killed by the flames or die when the mighty Lancaster hit the ground.

Gradually as the aircraft fell into a steeper dive, the flames were fanned nearer to Alkemede. He was fast being driven back towards his turret and it seemed that his end was near.

The Lancaster was at 18,000 feet when he made his decision. If he was going to die, he thought, he wanted to go quickly. He reached his gun turret and dived out!

The ice-cold night air hit Alkemede like a sledge hammer as he jumped. Then he was overcome by a tremendous feeling of peace and tranquility as he plunged towards the ground, actually thankful to be away from the scorching flames. Later, as his body gathered speed in the fall, reaching almost 120 miles an hour, he blacked out completely.

The seconds ticked by then he regained consciousness and glanced upwards, aware only of the now starlit sky. It was then that the startling truth dawned on him....he was no longer falling. He was on solid ground – and still alive. He was lying on his back in deep snow in the middle of a plantation of trees. Alkemede had fallen 18,000 feet without a parachute at 120 miles an hour and his fall had been broken by the trees and snow drifts. The staggering fact about this tremendous escape was that he suffered only minor bruises. He just couldn't believe his luck and pinched himself to make sure that he was indeed alive.

Some time later Alkemede was taken prisoner by the Germans and put into a prisoner of war camp where he told of his fantastic escape from almost certain death. The Germans wouldn't believe him at first but when they examined the crashed Lancaster they found the charred remains of his parachute still in its proper place. He was then as much of a hero with the Germans as he was with the Allied airmen in the camp.

By some miracle, Nicholas Alkemede had cheated death and his escape must be ranked amongst the most remarkable of the entire war.

• • • •

September 1940 saw the docks at Antwerp in Belgium crammed with specially constructed barges, waiting ready for the day when Adolf Hitler would launch 'Operation Sealion', the invasion of Britain. The German High Command had only to wait for the Luftwaffe's 'crushing defeat' of the Royal Air Force then hundreds of ships and barges would sweep across the Channel to Britain's shores and thousands of storm-troopers would invade the country.

That month in 1940 was the most crucial of the entire war for her. The Battle of Britain was at its height and while the pilots of Fighter Command warded off the hordes of German bombers sent to crush her into defeat, their comrades in Bomber Command attacked the barges clustered together in the ports along the north coast of German-occupied Belgium and France.

During one such raid, a young Scots wireless-operator/air-gunner, John Hannah, was to show the height of valour in the flak-ridden sky over Antwerp. Like all other bomber raids, this one began in the briefing room where the assembled bomber crews were given details of their target, weather conditions and the hazards they might encounter. Sergeant Hannah sat among the other airmen, listening intently to the intelligence reports given by the senior officers.

With a final 'Good Luck!' from the Commanding Officer, they all left the briefing room, chatting excitedly about the forthcoming raid. Antwerp had been hit before and the bomber boys knew that it was a tricky target. They knew only too well that they would fly into intense flak because the Germans had brought in a formidable concentration of guns to defend their precious barges against attack.

The twin-engined Hampden bombers they were to fly were the fastest the R.A.F. had in service at that time with a top speed of around 254 m.p.h. but even so they were still 'sitting ducks' for the German gunners.

Hannah, like all the other crewmen, had his share of pre-flight nerves as he heaved himself into the Hampden and clambered into his tiny compartment. Quickly he busied himself with his radio and soon the nerves were forgotten. Minutes later the ungainly Hampden bomber, with its dumpy body tapering off almost to a point at the tail, was lifting off the ground and climbing to join the formation of bombers already airborne. Then later as the formation droned towards Antwerp docks the whole sky erupted in a furious barrage of fire.

'Phew! They're sending it up thick and heavy,' thought Hannah, feeling the aircraft rock as shells exploded dangerously close to it. Shrapnel peppered the Hampden's fabric-covered fuselage as it droned resolutely on through the wall of flak, and the skipper had to fight to control the aircraft as it was tossed about the sky by near misses.

The Hampden was a curious aircraft in that each of the four members of the crew had his own tiny compartment. The pilot sat 'on top' of the aircraft while the navigator/bomb-aimer occupied the nose. An aluminium door separated them from Hannah in his little nook facing a bank of dials, knobs and switches and further back the rear gunner in his turret.

Hannah's Hampden nosed its way over the docks and suddenly as it did so, there was an ear-splitting bang and the aircraft lurched violently.

'We've been hit!' a voice yelled in the intercom. A shell had smashed into the Hampden. The rear-gunner's cockpit was ablaze. He had to act quickly. Throwing open his escape hatch he leapt out of the aircraft and parachuted safely to the ground. But the roaring fire swept through the fuselage fanned by the rushing air and soon reached Hannah's compartment.

'Damage report!' the Skipper said calmly over the inter-com.

'We're on fire!' Hannah replied. 'Looks bad.'

'Right! Stand by to bale out!'

Searing tongues of flame licked around Hannah and he grabbed the first thing that came to hand. It was his radio log book and he beat at the flames in a vain bid to put out the fire but it only raged more fiercely. To add a further hazard to an already desperate situation, exploding ammunition from the machine-guns in the rear cockpit whizzed and whined past Hannah as he fought the flames. Highly inflammable petrol gushed from punctured fuel tanks in both the wings and as the seconds ticked by the threat of a mighty explosion increased.

Hannah's log book was making no impression on the fire. He was fighting a losing battle. His only chance was to get to the fire extinguishers in the other compartment, behind the door. He grabbed the door handle and pulled but it was jammed. He heaved with all his might but it wouldn't budge.

The young Scotsman's plight was grim. In a last, desperate bid he threw himself at the door and smashed it down but in doing so he bounced back off it and fell headlong into the furnace of flame behind him. The scorching heat was unbearable. Twisting his body he wriggled free of the flames and leapt for the fire extinguishers. Grabbing one he turned on the fire, spraying the flames. Still the tongues of fire leapt towards him. The choking fumes were suffocating him.

Wind rushed into the bomb-bay through gaping holes and fanned the flames to a new, terrifying ferocity below Hannah's compartment. As he turned to grab another fire extinguisher, the metal floor beneath his feet began to melt, burning the soles of his flying boots. His head swam as fumes seeped into his disconnected oxygen pipe. Frantically he tore the oxygen mask from his face, fighting for breath, and instantly the cruel flames burned his skin. By then his gloves were burned through but in spite of this he gripped the fire extinguisher and sprayed the roaring fire. Gradually the sizzling spray began to tame the wall of fire. At last Hannah was winning the battle. As the extinguisher fizzled out, the flames were dying and Hannah was able to beat out the remaining pockets of fire with his hands and feet. But even then he was not finished. Certain pieces of equipment were still smouldering so he threw open the canopy over his compartment and tossed them out.

Only when the last flame had flickered and died did John Hannah drag himself to the pilot's cockpit. Pilot Officer Conner glanced round to see Hannah's blackened and burned face.

'Okay, skipper, the fire's out,' the Scot said coolly.

But the ordeal was far from over. Hannah discovered that

the navigator had baled out. This left them with a badly damaged bomber and no one to navigate them back to England. To make matters even worse, Hannah's radio was a charred wreck and all the navigating equipment had been destroyed. Hannah, his whole body aching from terrible burns, did all he could to help his skipper as he nursed the crippled Hampden back to base. It is a tribute to Conner's skill as a pilot that he managed to keep the bomber in the air at all.

Ambulances and fire engines raced to the crippled bomber as it touched down at the base. Hannah, his face, hands and feet severely burned, was rushed to hospital where skilled surgeons set about the grim task of repairing the damage done by the flames.

Months later, Hannah was able to leave hospital with his wounds healed following a long series of operations. For his courage, he was awarded the Victoria Cross and became the youngest airman ever to receive his country's highest decoration for valour.

• • • •

Luck plays a major part in survival in the sky and if anyone was ever lucky it was Sergeant William Stannard, a cockney air-gunner, who had one of the most remarkable escapes from death during a bomber raid in 1943.

Stannard owes his life to the man who designed the twin-engined Lockheed Ventura bomber. He was the rear-gunner in one such aircraft when, one day in 1943, the bomber came under heavy attack as it flew towards the Dutch coast. There was a thundering roar as the bomber burst into flames. The front of the fuselage was quickly ablaze and air rushing through great gashes in the aircraft forced the fire towards the rear gun turret where Stannard sat.

He gazed, horror-struck, as the wall of fire rushed towards him. His only chance of escape was to clip on his parachute and jump but when he glanced to where his parachute was stowed he saw only a bundle of charred fragments. It seemed that he was doomed to die the horrible death that bomber crews feared most of all. But just as the flames had almost reached Stannard's cockpit, there was a violent explosion.

The whole aircraft rocked violently and in an instant, Stannard found himself gazing into space. Three quarters of the bomber had fallen away, leaving Stannard trapped in his tail gun turret!

'This is it,' he thought.

He expected that in a few seconds the tail would tilt and hurtle towards the ground to smash into a thousand bits. But soon, to his astonishment, he realised that, instead of plunging towards the ground, the tail was actually *flying* on an even keel, gently floating towards the earth. With the tail-plane supporting what was left of the fuselage, the tail was acting just like a glider.

Stannard peered over the ragged edge of the torn fuselage and watched the Dutch coastline come slowly up towards him. The cool air rushed in and fanned his burning face. The relief was sensational and the peace almost dream-like. But the closer the tail came to the ground, the faster the ground rushed up. He braced himself for the impact and seconds later the tail-plane hit a tree with an almighty crash. Stannard was tossed forwards and knocked unconscious when his 'aircraft' jarred to a halt. He had landed near a mansion house in the grounds of a big estate.

The whole fantastic episode had been witnessed by the gardener working in the grounds and he rushed to the tree and pulled Stannard's limp body from the wreckage.

Some time later, Stannard came to and found himself in the sumptuous surroundings of the mansion drawing room. His body ached all over and he could barely see but he could just detect the blurred figures of people fussing around him. A glass of wine was put in his hand and he gulped it down thankfully.

He leaned back in his chair and slowly the blurred figures began to take on a more definite shape. He could see a lady there with a kindly face and a man in working clothes who was the gardener who had rescued him. Becoming aware that there were more people in the room, he turned his head slowly. There standing beside him were a Luftwaffe officer and a member of the Gestapo (the German Secret Police). He knew then what was in store for him. He had faced death and survived, thanks to a lucky fluke in his bomber's design. Now he was to be marched off to a prisoner of war camp, but nevertheless he was still, beyond the faintest shadow of doubt, the luckiest man alive.

•   •   •   •

Perhaps the most terrifying ordeal by fire came when airmen who had had to bale out from their aircraft pulled the ripcords of their parachutes only to find the silk canopy above their heads ablaze. A burning canopy almost certainly meant a horrible death. Sergeant Norman Jackson was to know all the terror of that situation one night in 1943.

Jackson was the flight engineer in a Lancaster bomber which droned over Germany through the darkness on that fateful night. Sitting in front of a mass of dials which monitored the performance of each of its four powerful Merlin engines, Jackson satisfied himself that all was well. Roaring through the air at 200 m.p.h. the Lancaster, one of a huge formation, closed in on the target, Schweinfurt.

The pilot steadied the aircraft for the run in on the target while the bomb-aimer in the nose peered through the bomb-sight. The Lanc was now at its most vulnerable, flying straight and level while Jackson's eyes darted over the dials, checking the engines.

A few seconds later the bomb doors clanged open, revealing the clusters of bombs in the bomb-bay and tension mounted as the target loomed up ahead. Suddenly the bomb-aimer's crisp voice yelled out over the intercom....

'Bombs away!'

The huge Lancaster soared higher into the air as the bombs fell away from the aircraft and whistled down towards the target. Eager eyes watched as the bombs exploded on the target sending up a mountainous mushroom of smoke.

The crew was jubilant — but their relaxation was to be short-lived. The pilot heaved on the control column and the Lancaster climbed away from the burning target. Then, like a thunderbolt, a German fighter streaked in on the Lanc, spraying it with bullets. As the bullets drew their tracery on the fuselage, Jackson was hit on the head and blood poured from his wound, blinding him in one eye.

The fighter shot past the Lanc and the crew quickly took stock of the situation. The starboard wing between the inner engine and the fuselage was blazing like a torch. There were fuel tanks in that wing and if the fire was not put out quickly, the aircraft would blow up. Jackson did not hesitate. Scrambling to the pilot's cockpit, he tapped his skipper on the shoulder:

'Starboard wing's on fire, skipper. I'm going to have a crack at putting it out. I'm going out on the wing.'

'You'll never make it,' the pilot shouted over the roar of the engines. But by then Jackson was back in the fuselage and clipping on his parachute pack. He stuffed three small fire extinguishers into his flying suit then crawled forward to jettison the escape hatch above the pilot.

Jackson hauled himself out of the cockpit onto the top of the fuselage and was immediately almost blown away by the howling 200 m.p.h. slipstream. Gripping any projection he could find, he began easing himself along the fuselage. The release ring on his parachute must have caught on the fuselage for, seconds later, his parachute spilled out of the pack and the canopy billowed back into the cockpit. Three members of the crew grabbed the silk canopy and held on to it for dear life. Just then Jackson lost his hold and fell onto the wing — right into the heart of the fire. He grabbed a burning air intake and held on with flames licking around him, which burned his face and hands and set his clothes alight. The pain was almost unbearable but he held on.

As if his plight were not desperate enough, the German fighter attacked again, raking the wing with bullets. Jackson was hit again in the back and in the legs. The stinging pain made him lose his grip on the air intake and he was whipped off the wing by the slipstream. The crew watched horrified as Jackson dangled in the slipstream behind the Lancaster — four miles above the ground.

'There's only one thing for it,' one of the crewmen said. 'We'll have to let him go. We can't get him back. At least his parachute should save him.'

Slowly they paid out the rigging lines and canopy but as it slipped out of the cockpit, it caught fire in the inferno on the wing. Jackson floated earthwards with the hungry flames eating away at the canopy above his head. As more and more of the parachute was burned away he fell faster and faster towards the ground. The darkened earth rushed up towards him then he hit the ground with a thud, breaking one leg and the ankle of the other. Pain shot through his body as he lay, dazed, on the ground.

Jackson knew he could die where he lay if he didn't get help. With heroic determination, he began pulling himself along the ground. Every movement of his body was agonising and the pain grew worse as he progressed. After what seemed like an eternity, he reached a village and was taken prisoner.

With bullet wounds in his head, back and legs, half blind, badly burned and with a broken leg and ankle, Norman Jackson spent the next ten months in hospital recovering from his terrible wounds. Then when he was discharged from hospital he was put in a prisoner of war camp. There his fighting spirit showed itself again. He tried to escape but was recaptured. Disappointed but undaunted, he tried again and this time he made it, reaching the advancing American army. Jackson was sent back to England where his amazing story was told. Not long after, he was summoned to Buckingham Palace and there decorated with the Victoria Cross.

● ● ● ●

Many hundreds of airmen were killed during the last war when their aircraft were enveloped in fire and spun down out of control into the ground. There must be countless stories of heroism which can never be told because no one lived to tell them. The following story might well have become yet another of these untold tales of courage had it not been for the daring of a Canadian pilot.

One of the most boring duties given to pilots in the Second World War was flying the huge flying-boats that scoured the oceans and seas for enemy surface craft and submarines. It required infinite patience. One can visualise a vast expanse of ocean and a comparatively small aeroplane searching for an equally small ship. That was the unenviable task given to David Hornell, a pilot in the Royal Canadian Air Force.

Before the outbreak of the war, Hornell, who was a native of Toronto, worked with a rubber company and when Britain was plunged into war and Canada followed, Hornell volunteered for the R.C.A.F. After qualifying as a pilot, he was posted to a squadron flying Cansos flying-boats. Operating from Vancouver, he piloted his flying-boat far out into the Pacific for hours and hours on end while his crew scanned the ocean with binoculars searching for the briefest glimpse of a periscope cutting through the waves. He longed for action, anything to break the monotony of flying continually over a seemingly endless sea. But it seemed that he was destined to go through the war without firing a shot in anger.

Then, to make matters worse, he was taken off operational duties and posted to an air base where he became a test pilot, still flying the old Cansos flying-boats. It was not until 1943 that he was posted back to operational duties, this time in Iceland. But still it was the Cansos he had to fly in the same old routine of sweeping the sea in the hope of spotting a sub.

Beneath the waves of the Atlantic lurked the U-boats, operating in wolf packs, as they were called, wreaking havoc amongst convoys of merchantmen bringing supplies from Canada and America to Britain. Day after day, the U-boats made their sneak attacks and sent more ships to the bottom of the ocean. Hornell's patience was wearing thin. He cursed his luck that he had no means of striking back at the enemy.

For almost a year he had to wait. Then on a summer day in 1944, he and his crew took off from their base and headed out to sea. The Cansos droned on over the sea while the crew peered out through their binoculars. For hours they ploughed on uneventfully. Hornell yawned as he lifted his eyes from the instrument panel in front of him to the wilderness of sea. He glanced out on the port side of his cockpit and his heart almost stopped. Far to the left he could see the unmistakable cigar-shaped outline of a U-boat on the surface.

'U-boat on the port side!' Hornell yelled excitedly through the intercom. 'Stand by to attack!'

Instantly the seven-man crew dashed to their battle stations. Hornell wheeled the Cansos round towards the U-boat. But as the flying-boat homed in on the enemy submarine, the German captain in the conning tower caught sight of the aeroplane.

A klaxon sounded and the gun's-crew darted out of the conning tower and made for the heavy gun mounted forward of the tower. Hurriedly they wheeled the barrel round towards the diving flying-boat.

'Fire!' the captain yelled, ducking for cover behind the metal rim of the conning tower.

The gun roared and a shell exploded alongside the Cansos, lashing it with shrapnel and puncturing the fuselage. The shells came fast and furious along with a withering hail of machine-gun fire. The German gunners had found their mark.

Bullets riddled the fuselage while the shells continued to burst all around the Cansos but Hornell gritted his teeth and held the Cansos on course with his eyes fixed on the growing shape of the U-boat.

Then suddenly a shell crashed into the starboard engine. Instantly it caught fire and flames licked over the wing. Hornell cursed his luck and fought to keep the aeroplane flying. Then suddenly the whole aircraft lurched as the engine fell off and dropped into the sea. The wing was now blazing furiously and with the loss of power from one engine, Hornell had to use all his flying skill to keep the plane from heeling over and plunging into the sea. Within seconds the flames could reach the fuel tanks and blow them to bits but still he flew on, his eyes intent on the U-boat.

'We've gone this far. I'm not breaking off the attack now!' he muttered.

The blazing flying-boat careered on towards the U-boat and Hornell shouted to the crew to stand by the depth charges. More bullets lashed the aeroplane slashing some of the control lines. There was no turning back now. Even if he wanted to, Hornell could not have got the Cansos out of the dive. They were doomed to crash but Hornell was determined that he was going to get the U-boat before he ditched in the sea.

Now the Cansos was only fifty yards from the U-boat and the German gunners were pumping shells into her. Fire was sweeping along her wing towards Hornell's cockpit as bits were blasted off the fuselage by the barrage of shells. Hornell held his breath as his plane plunged crazily towards the submarine. Then just a fraction of a second before the Cansos shot over the sub, Hornell released the depth charges. With a blinding flash they exploded on the deck of the submarine sending twisted and torn metal hurtling into the air and into the belly of the flying-boat. The Cansos gave a last lurch in the air then tilted over. The blast of the depth charges literally lifted the submarine into the air then it plunged back into the sea, a tangled wreck.

Hornell battled with the controls of the aircraft. It bounced off the surface of the sea then rose into the air again. Still the flames spread over the wing and licked into the cockpit. Then suddenly the plane hit the water and the crew were hurled about inside the fuselage. The whole of the starboard side was ablaze and the crew scrambled out through the gun-port on the port side. Hornell and his co-pilot, Denomy, threw open the hatch above their heads and scrambled out onto the top of the fuselage only to be met by the roar of flames. Instantly they leapt into the sea and made for an already inflated rubber dinghy. It was then that Hornell learned the horrible truth. They had only one tiny dinghy between the eight of them. The other had been burnt in the fire on the wing where it was stored. There was only one thing for it. They would have to take turns at going into the water.

By then the U-boat had sunk leaving only bits of wreckage scattered about in the water and slowly the flying-boat too slid beneath the waves. The dinghy was now alone. The prospect of rescue seemed remote and after the excitement of battle Hornell and his crew were exhausted. They shivered continuously as a biting wind swept across the sea. The waves grew mountainous and the men in the water held on to the dinghy with all the strength they could muster. Then a wave crashed down on the dinghy, capsizing it and tossing the occupants into the water. They fought furiously to right the dinghy and after a bitter fight against the waves succeeded. Four of them clambered back in. The duel with the elements sapped all their remaining strength. The hours dragged by and the dinghy capsized yet again. Miraculously they managed to right it once more but not long after, St. Laurent, one of the flight engineers, died. Hornell tried desperately to raise their spirits but he was fighting a losing battle.

Then, as all seemed lost, they heard the drone of aircraft engines. Hornell looked up to see an air/sea rescue aircraft. It roared over them and dropped a boat. At last they had a chance. But their hearts sank when the boat fell almost a quarter of a mile away. Absolutely exhausted as they were, they had no hope of reaching it. None of them had the strength to swim or even paddle the dinghy that distance. A short while later the other engineer, Matheson, died.

All through the night they waited until, more than twenty hours later a rescue launch ploughed through the waves towards them. At the sight of the boat, Hornell lapsed into unconsciousness and one by one the members of the crew were lifted aboard the boat. Though the boat raced back to base Hornell never regained consciousness. He died some time later. The surviving members of the crew unquestionably owed their lives to Hornell's spirit in the dinghy when all seemed lost. Later Squadron Leader David Hornell was posthumously awarded the Victoria Cross.

16
They Flew against the Flying-Bomb

On the 12th of June 1944, a new and terrifying sound reached the ears of Londoners as they went about their business in the crowded streets. The rasping *burp burp* of a motor in the air could be heard. They looked up, scanning the sky for a sight of an aeroplane and saw a strange cigar-shaped aircraft with stubby wings flash across the sky. Then suddenly the motor stopped and the aircraft seemed to falter in the sky then dip its nose towards the ground. Those watching believed the pilot must be in trouble as the aircraft plummeted down in a spin then hit the ground. There followed a mighty explosion as 1,870 pounds of high-explosive blew up, wrecking everything around it.

The horrified onlookers had not, as they thought, witnessed the death of a piloted aircraft but the beginning of a reign of Nazi terror which was to bring death and destruction to their city. The first of Hitler's terror weapons, the V-1 flying bomb, had fallen on London – and there were thousands more to come.

In the weeks that followed that first attack, more than 100 flying-bombs descended on England *every day* demolishing hundreds of buildings and killing over 6,000 people. The death toll and destruction wrought by these flying-bombs might have been much greater had it not been for the courage and daring of a handful of secret agents and the fighter and bomber pilots of the Royal Air Force.

The story of the V-1 (an abbreviation for *Vergeltunsgwaffe* 1 – a retaliation weapon No.1) began even before the outbreak of the Second World War when German scientists, during the 1920s worked on perfecting a pulse-jet engine which would propel a pilotless aircraft filled with high-explosives to its target. Why, they reasoned, should a German air force risk the lives of its bomber pilots over enemy territory when it could launch its bombs with impunity from the security of its own territory, and carry out a bombardment of the enemy without fear of losing a single German? This then was the concept but it was to be a long time before the weapon was perfected. The conventional German air force was built up to tremendous strength during the years before the outbreak of war, with the Luftwaffe chiefs concentrating on the production of bombers and fighters, but in the backrooms the scientists persisted with their work, trying and testing their inventions until in 1942, when the war was barely three years old, they had achieved what they all agreed was the perfect design.

The flying-bomb which ultimately evolved from their experiments was cigar-shaped with the short and stubby main wings set midships of the fuselage and a lateral pair of even shorter wings at the tail. The propulsion unit which housed the pulse-jet was contained in a tube mounted above the tail. The complete machine weighed slightly more than two tons, being constructed in the main of pressed steel. It was 25.4 feet in length with a wing span of 17.7 feet. The motor was a single Argus pulse-jet engine, which developed a thrust of 740 pounds giving the bomb a cruising speed of around 400 miles an hour at a height of 3000 feet.

The bomb had many advantages, not the least of which was its operating height. Flying at 3000 feet, it was too low and fast to be shot down by the heavy anti-aircraft guns which were most affective against high-flying targets and too high to be hit by the light anti-aircraft guns.

The prototype of the flying-bomb was ready for firing in December 1942 and after a great many test-firings was ready to go into production by the middle of 1943. By this time it had been developed and modified to such an extent that it could be set to explode within half a mile of its target, a truly staggering accomplishment.

With the war generally running in favour of the Allies, who had by then invaded Italy and won the North African campaign, Hitler at last saw his new terror weapon as the only means of reversing his fortunes and systematically bringing Britain to her knees. The development and production of the flying-bomb had taken place at the rocket research establishment at Peenemünde, a top secret base and the hub of the German scientists' work on secret weapons of all descriptions.

Thousands of Germans were put to work on the production of the terror weapon and vast stores of them were massed for the day when Hitler would unleash them against the British capital. Even more workers were busy constructing launching sites along the north coast of Europe. It was Hitler's intention to launch upwards of a thousand of these bombs against London *every day* beginning in December 1943. It does not take a great deal of imagination to envisage the result of such an aerial onslaught, had it been allowed to happen.

Special German Luftwaffe units were formed and trained to operate the V-1s while 40,000 labourers worked day and night to complete the launching sites, meanwhile the flying-bombs flowed off the assembly lines.

British intelligence agents in Europe had heard whispers of the development of a German secret weapon which would turn the tide of the war but they did not know what it was. The credit for its discovery must go to a Polish school teacher who, early in the war, following the German invasion of Poland, had been sent to a forced labour camp near Peenemünde where he was put to work constructing concrete roads and gun emplacements.

Before being transported to Germany a friend had warned this teacher to keep his eyes and ears open. The friend was a member of the Polish Underground Movement and was in contact with London and anxious to send to Britain all the information he could muster which might help the Allied cause. The teacher remembered this when, one day, he and another worker were taken off their normal duties and detailed to go to the top-secret site at Peenemünde to carry out sanitary duties, cleaning out toilets and washrooms. One morning as they were transporting some rubbish to the incinerator, they passed a large shed and noticed that the door had been left ajar. They casually looked inside and there to their astonishment, they saw a strange aircraft standing on trestles, one of a kind they had never seen before. The point that struck them as most odd about this machine was that it had no cockpit for the pilot and no propeller. This gave the two men food for thought and the teacher realised that this snippet of information could well be of use to his friend in Poland. Within a few days, the teacher managed to send a message to his friend telling him of what he had seen and the news was at once relayed to London. The Intelligence Service in London was extremely interested in this piece of information which confirmed their suspicions and they eagerly asked for more.

The bits of the puzzle began to fall into place and make sense, for rumours of strange constructions being built in France, Belgium, and Holland had already reached the ears of the Intelligence chiefs in Britain.

While the Polish teacher continued to get as much information as he could, there was another patriot in France. He was Michel Hollard, a Frenchman in his forties who worked as an industrial designer. He, like the Polish teacher had learned to keep his ear to the ground and since the fall of France had been sending vital information back to England via Switzerland. He had fed the Intelligence Service with information about the location of Luftwaffe airfields, submarine bases, gun emplacements, troop movements etc. etc., by slipping across the Swiss border on more than forty occasions to meet a British agent located there.

Because of the nature of his job, Hollard was comparatively free to travel the length and breadth of France and in doing so was in a perfect position to see what was going on and also to pick up tit-bits of information from agents whom he himself had recruited.

Hollard's most remarkable discovery resulted from one of his agents overhearing two building contractors talking about some construction work they were involved in which demanded vast amounts of concrete. The agent's curiosity was roused and he reported what he had heard to Hollard.

Hollard puzzled over how he could get more information about these çonstructions, then hit on the idea of taking the bold approach. The following day he travelled to Rouen, where one of the sites was under construction and, posing as a representative of a religious organisation, approached an official of a local employment office. He asked if he could be allowed to help look after the spiritual welfare of local workers and enquired if there were any large building sites nearby where he could begin his work. The official readily told him that there was indeed one at Auffey, about twenty miles from Rouen.

Wasting no time, Hollard made for Auffey, where he saw the site. He donned a set of workman's clothes and 'borrowing' a wheelbarrow entered the site, accepted by the guard on the main gate as one of the many workmen who continually went in and out. Once inside he enquired of the workmen apparently casually, what they were building and was told that they were constructing garages.

'Very strange place to have garages,' Hollard thought. 'And very robust constructions too. Now why would the Germans want garages twenty miles from the nearest town?' he wondered.

Hollard made his way round the site until he came to a long concrete ramp with a guideline running right up the centre of it. For a moment he was puzzled until he realised in which direction the ramp was pointing. He produced a compass from his pocket and soon discovered that the ramp was aimed directly at London. This of course could have been purely coincidental but it struck Hollard as interesting. He then made a few more discreet enquiries of the workmen and found that they were complaining of being forced to work round the clock so as to get the site completed quickly. 'The Germans wouldn't go all out like this just to put up some garages,' Hollard thought. 'This is something for London.'

Wasting no time, he got off to London all the information he could muster about the site. There the Intelligence men put two and two together. The pilotless plane they had heard about from the Polish teacher would have to be launched from somewhere and probably from a ramp. This they thought must be the link and urgent messages were sent to Hollard to get as much information as possible about the location of any more sites.

Hollard swept into action and recruiting three other agents, he and his men began a systematic tour of northern France where they found more and more of these sites dotted along the coastline. The Germans' intention was now obvious – a second blitz on London.

During his investigations, Hollard not only got the exact locations of these sites but also a complete blueprint of a typical site, indicating the positions of the buildings where the bombs were to be housed as well as the position of the ramp. After a series of breathtaking experiences, Hollard finally succeeded in smuggling the blueprint across the Swiss border hidden in a sack of potatoes.

Even before the information had arrived from Hollard, the R.A.F. was planning to strike at the heart of flying-bomb production with a vast raid on Peenemünde, where not only was the flying-bomb being developed but also the more powerful, destructive and unstoppable V-2 rocket.

On the night of August 17th/18th, 1943, six hundred R.A.F. bombers roared across the North Sea and pounded Peenemünde with high-explosive bombs. The following morning the site was a scene of utter devastation. Most of the buildings had been razed to the ground, many of the top German scientists involved in rocket production were dead and many of the detailed plans for the construction of the rockets and flying-bombs destroyed by fire. Of the 600 bombers which took part in the raid 41 were lost but this was a small price to pay for bringing German rocket production virtually to a halt. Peenemünde was now useless as a base to work from and Hitler had to move the research establishment deeper into Germany.

The British, however, were not content to leave things at that. Great hordes of bombers swept across the Channel to rain down bombs on the rocket launching sites and thanks to the valiant work done by Hollard, they fell where they did the greatest damage. Armed with a revolutionary new bomb-sight and knowing exactly where to hit the sites for the maximum effect, Bomber Command completely destroyed almost all of them.

The Germans had received a tremendous setback and the

date of their great bombardment of London had to be postponed. However, after several thwarted attempts to rebuild the launching sites, they devised a new type of *metal* launch ramp which was less obvious from the air and much more easily camouflaged.

This put the Germans temporarily ahead in the duel, and meanwhile their store of flying-bombs was mounting. The R.A.F. had delayed the operation six months, but by June 1944, the Luftwaffe was ready to begin its attack. Still, although Hitler had boasted that he could rain a thousand bombs down on the British capital every day, the R.A.F. had done its job so well that he could actually launch only 100 to 150 a day.

By this time, however, the invasion of Europe had begun. There was no time to lose. The Luftwaffe could no longer wait for the vast stocks of bombs that had been promised. Hitler demanded instant action. He wanted London reduced to ruins in the hope that the Allies would sue for peace. His Luftwaffe commanders urged him to aim the bombs at the invasion beaches in Normandy to stem the tide of Allied troops and equipment pouring into Europe, or at least at the south coast ports in England to stop the flow of supplies before they reached France. But Hitler would not be swayed from his course. He was determined on the complete destruction of London. Had he taken the advice of his Chiefs of Staff, the invasion of Europe might have ended in utter catastrophe for the Allies. Instead, he gave the orders to begin the bombardment.

The first 'great' flying-bomb attack on London, on June 12th, went off like a damp squib. Wave after wave of bombs were planned to rain down on the capital but instead of the thousand bombs Hitler had threatened to send, only *ten* were actually fired, owing to many of the sites still being unserviceable. Of the ten that were fired only four reached England and of these only one hit the capital. If this was Hitler's threatened terror weapon in action, then there was little to worry about, many people thought. But the bombardment was yet to start in earnest.

After a lull of three days, the German Luftwaffe began launching the bombs at a rate of between 100 and 200 a day. Many of them failed to reach England but those that did hit their targets caused terrible damage. Casualties rose at an alarming rate and something had to be done quickly if Hitler's threat of destroying the morale of London were not to be fulfilled.

More and more anti-aircraft guns were sent to the south coast of England and a great string of barrage balloons strung along the coast. Between them these precautions exacted a certain toll on the bombs as they winged their way over the coast but what was to prove the most effective deterrent was the R.A.F. fighter pilot in the new Tempest fighter though attacks of this kind were not without their dangers.

To begin with the R.A.F. pilots flew at the flying-bombs and raked them with cannon fire making them explode, but the resulting explosion often caused serious damage to the fighter. Then another more cunning way of combating these bombs was devised; one which required all the fighter pilots' skill.

On sighting a flying-bomb the pilot would get alongside it and fly with his wing-tip just below that of the flying-bomb. Then he would raise his wing-tip so that it touched the flying-bomb's wing. The result was that the bomb became unstable and veered off course to plunge earthwards and explode harmlessly in the English Channel. Many hundreds of bombs which would otherwise have wreaked havoc in England were destroyed in this way. One flying-bomb 'ace', Squadron Leader Joseph Berry, succeeded in destroying no less than *sixty* flying-bombs, fifty-seven of them at night! In one mission he actually destroyed *seven* bombs.

By the first of September, no fewer than 8600 bombs had been launched at London. Many failed to reach their target, some because of faulty guidance systems, others because of anti-aircraft fire but mostly because of the R.A.F's activities with the Tempest, Spitfire and Mosquito fighters. The beginning of September saw the end of the first phase of attacks but there were more to come....

The Germans were worried about the number of bombs which did not reach their targets because of faulty guidance systems. Something had to be done about the appalling wastage of bombs and a new system was devised using the Heinkel He.111 as a transporter for the bombs which could be launched from the bombers when near the target. Special squadrons were formed, equipped with the out-dated bomber and their job was to carry the bomb to within a given distance of the target then launch it and dash back to base.

The principle of 'stand-off' bombing (as this was known) was good in theory but it had one serious disadvantage. The aircraft used was slow and vulnerable to attack by fighters and anti-aircraft because it was slowed down even more by the excessive load it had to carry. The result was that the Heinkels became 'easy meat' for the R.A.F. fighters and seventy-seven of them were shot down, many at night.

The flying-bombs continued to be sent over by the conventional method but in ever decreasing numbers. The Allied armies were creeping forward across Europe towards the Reich and as they gained more ground they captured more and more launching sites. As the Luftwaffe had to withdraw further, the accuracy of the bombs was considerably reduced. In one attack intended for Southampton, the bombs were so wildly off target that the defenders thought the attack had been intended for Portsmouth, almost 15 miles away!

From one site in Holland 275 bombs were launched by the S.S. but the defenders of London had become so expert at shooting down the bombs that only 13 of them actually got through to the target.

When these attacks finally came to an end in March 1945, over 10,000 had been launched at England of which 7500 reached the island. Almost half of these were destroyed before getting to their targets, others missed completely and 2500 succeeded in hitting their targets. The damage done by these bombs was vast. 6184 civilians were killed and a further 18,000 injured but had it not been for the combined efforts of R.A.F. Bomber and Fighter Commands, the total would have been infinitely greater.

They, in fact, destroyed no fewer than 1300 of the bombs before they got to their target.

17
The Bang Seat

During the First World War, many Allied pilots perished needlessly in crippled or burning aircraft because of the short-sightedness and naivety of their High Command. The one device which might have saved them from death was denied them.....the parachute. For reasons which today sound almost unbelievable, the 'top-brass' gave a flat 'no' to repeated requests for the supply of parachutes.

It was not as if parachutes were not available. As far back as the 1880s, tests had been carried out with early parachute designs and proved successful. By the beginning of the First World War the parachute had reached such a state of perfection that the makers could guarantee almost one hundred per cent reliability. Exhaustive tests had taken place in America, France and Britain to prove and substantiate the claim. Why, then, was not every Allied pilot equipped with the means to save his life if he got into difficulties? The reasons given by the High Command were almost beyond belief.

They claimed that carrying a parachute would impair the performance of the fighting aircraft. In the first couple of years of the war, there was perhaps an element of truth in this, since the aeroplanes that the aviators flew could barely carry the pilot, let alone a gun with which to fight and a parachute as well. But when better aircraft were provided later, the justification for this argument was no longer valid. By then the aircraft were perfectly capable of carrying parachute equipment as well as all the necessities of war without affecting their performance.

The most ludicrous assertions of all were based on purely psychological foundations. The suggestion was that, equipped with a parachute, the pilot might lose his nerve if things got 'too hot' for him and abandon his aircraft. The very suggestion that this might happen angered fighter pilots so much that aces like Mannock and McCudden, whose courage in the air no one could doubt, set themselves up as spokesmen in favour of the issue of parachutes. Alas, even such men as these could not budge officialdom from its entrenched position and the utterly senseless loss of Allied airmen continued unabated. In fact, the reverse of the High Command's argument would have been nearer the truth. A pilot equipped with a parachute, who knew he had a fair chance of escape if his aircraft were crippled, was much more likely to take real chances than one who was without a parachute.

The result of the stubbornness shown by those in power was that many young airmen who might well have lived to fight another day were lost. This was appallingly wasteful, since pilots were infinitely more valuable than planes. Materials to build aircraft were fairly easily obtainable but men capable of being taught to fly them were not and a pilot needed months of training. Despite these obvious facts not a single Allied airman was officially supplied with a parachute during the whole war.

Fortunately the men who commanded the Royal Air Force between the wars and during the Second World War were much more enlightened than their predecessors and knew the value of their aircrew. By their directions every airman was trained in the use of the parachute. The parachute also took on a new importance when it began to be used as a means of getting airborne troops to the battlefields.

Great fleets of aircraft flew over enemy territory dropping paratroops with their supplies by the thousand.

Even more sinister uses of the parachute were made during the war when British and Allied secret agents were dropped at dead of night into the heart of enemy territory to organise spy-rings and sabotage.

As the war progressed and faster and more efficient aircraft came into service with the air forces of the world, those concerned with air safety were faced with a problem. It was one thing pulling back the canopy of, say, a Spitfire, travelling at 300 m.p.h. and jumping out, but it was quite another thing getting out of the cockpit of an aircraft travelling at 500 m.p.h. At high speeds it became almost impossible for a pilot to get out of his cockpit at all. Often he was forced back in again by the strength of the slipstream and even if he did succeed in getting free of the cockpit, the likelihood was that he would be hurled back against the tail and killed rather than drop clear. Somehow the experts had to devise a way of getting the pilot out of the aircraft safely and above all quickly before he opened his parachute.

When jet aircraft came into service with the R.A.F., the need for a better type of escape system became even more urgent. A number of possible schemes were put forward and tested. The most promising one consisted of a long metal arm which lay along the top of the fuselage, its rear end anchored just forward of the tail fin while its front end jutted into the pilot's cockpit. This front end had a u-shaped hand which slotted into rings on the pilot's harness and the whole contraption was secured in the cockpit by a powerful spring. The idea was that when the pilot pulled the release, the arm would be released, pull him clean out of the cockpit and throw him clear of the aircraft. Tests were carried out with models and they proved successful. However a change of policy within the Air Ministry indicated that the new escape system would be required, not just for existing aircraft but for those very much faster machines which were at that time only on the drawing board. This meant that the 'swinging arm' project had to be abandoned. Something even more effective had to be found.

It was obvious to the scientists and technicians working in this field that the best alternative to the swinging arm was one where the pilot and the seat in which he was sitting were ejected together out of the cockpit. The only sensible and effective way of doing that was by the use of an explosive charge which would blast pilot and seat clear of the aircraft after the canopy had been ejected. Once free of the plane the pilot and the seat would part company leaving the pilot to float gently to the ground by conventional parachute.

In theory, the idea looked good but there was still a long way to go. No one at that time knew what effect the sudden thrust caused by the ejection would have upon the unfortunate pilot. The part of his anatomy which would be most prone to damage during 'blast off' would be his spinal column so this meant that the explosive charge could not be too great, otherwise the spine would be fractured. It was pretty obvious that the medical men would have to be closely involved in the development of the ejector seat and experts were called in to assist. Somehow they had to determine how much thrust the body could withstand without injury.

A whole series of detailed tests was arranged with the use of a special rig which had a tall vertical 'slide' with a rail running up its length. Attached to this slide was the prototype ejector seat which upon the discharge of an explosive charge at the base, would shoot up the rail. To begin with tests were carried out using dummies in the shape of sand bags which were shot to the top of the ramp. A great deal of vital information was gained in this way. Experiments were carried out like that for four days in January 1945. But the acid test had yet to come. A volunteer had to be found who would be willing to sit in the seat and be rocketed up the ramp. At last a 'guinea-pig' was found in the robust shape of Benny Lynch, a very well-built fitter. On 24th January, 1945, the courageous Lynch was strapped into the prototype seat which had been specially designed by James Martin, the man who can rightly be called the 'father' of the ejector seat.

It was with some trepidation that the onlookers watched the straps being tightened round Lynch's bulky frame as he sat there on the 'powder-keg'. The explosive charge which was being used was a relatively small one but nothing quite like this had ever been tried before with a human, so anything could happen. As the watching technicians retreated to a safe distance, Lynch must have felt himself rather like the pointer in one of those test-your-strength devices at a side-show.

With an almighty bang, the charge exploded and Lynch felt a jar as he shot upwards – to a height of four feet eight inches. The first test had succeeded. Gradually more and more powerful charges were put in the seat, driving Lynch higher and higher until he reached a height of almost twelve feet. It was then that things began to go wrong. For the first time since the tests had started, Lynch complained of back pains. Things were reaching a critical point.

The tests continued until another of the guinea-pigs was seriously injured, breaking his back. James Martin was in a quandary. The test in which the man had been injured had been exactly the same as the others. The reason for the trouble appeared to have something to do with the individual man's spine. Martin, determined to discover why one man should be affected and not others, decided to go on a crash course as to how and why the spine works. He attended a number of operations on the spine to widen his knowledge and also obtained a human spine, taken from a skeleton. This he studied, with his medical advisers, subjecting it to innumerable mechanical tests. Martin's investigations enabled him to calculate just how much acceleration the spine could withstand, and with this determined, he set about making certain changes in design to his ejector seat. He altered the position of the foot rests which helped keep the spinal column straight and introduced a two cartridge gun into his seat instead of the normal single charge. The first cartridge was fairly low powered, just strong enough to start the seat moving, while the second cartridge had a much more powerful charge which would give the seat the speed necessary for it to blast clear of the plane. Martin had realised that if the acceleration were gradual to begin with, this lessened the chances of spinal injury.

In all, 180 'live' shots were carried out on the ramp, then a Boulton Paul Defiant was specially converted and fitted with an ejector seat. Using the Defiant as the launch pad, many tests were carried out at speeds of up to 300 miles an hour. The results were highly successful.

It was then decided to go a stage further and a Meteor jet was specially converted and used in the first instance as a static launch pad, then later for airborne tests. The logical next step was a live, human ejection from a jet aircraft and Benny Lynch again volunteered his services.

On the 24th July, 1946, Lynch took off in a Meteor fighter and when the aircraft reached a height of 8000 feet he ejected himself. The blast of the two cartridges sent him and the seat careering into the sky, free of the aircraft, which was then travelling at an airspeed of 320 miles an hour. Everything worked perfectly. The seat and Lynch parted company as planned and the parachute opened. He floated gently towards the ground to a perfect landing. It was a smiling Lynch who was greeted to cheers by the waiting onlookers on the ground. He had become the first man in Britain ever to eject from a moving aircraft. This was what everyone had been waiting for.

The results of that test led to certain modifications being made to the seat that Lynch had used so that mass production could begin. Then more dummy tests were made with the modified seat and the few teething troubles that arose, cleared up.

Martin was taking absolutely no chances. He was determined to perfect the design before it went into mass production and again, on the 29th August, 1947, Lynch made another ejection from the Meteor, this time from a height of 12,000 feet at an air speed of 420 m.p.h. Again he made a perfect ejection and landing, all of which proved the effectiveness of the modifications Martin had made. From then on, Lynch made more ejections, some thirty in all, contributing valuable information to air safety. For his services he was awarded the British Empire Medal in 1948.

The next step in the process was to standardise the ejector seat, so that it could be easily fitted into the aircraft currently in service at that time like the Meteor, Wyvern, Attacker and Canberra jet bomber. The Fleet Air Arm's Sea Hawk and the R.A.F's Venom jet fighter which were flowing off the production line, were also fitted with the revolutionary seat.

There was, however, one major drawback to the early models of the seat; their operation was not fully automatic. After ejection, the pilot had to unfasten his seat belt while he hurtled towards the ground, allow the seat to fall away then pull the rip-cord of his parachute. This had obvious dangers in that a pilot who was injured might be unable to go through these processes. Indeed, the aircraft might be too low to allow him *time* to go through them.

Martin and his team got down to work to see how they could best solve the problem. He had not only to design an automatic system but also one which could be incorporated in the seats that were already in use. Eventually, a new design emerged from the drawing board. He had invented a Time Release Mechanism which was fitted onto the side beam of the seat. The release was tripped by a static line as the seat was ejected out of the aircraft and the mechanism ran for a full five seconds before it released the seat harness by pulling on a cable which rotated the face plate on the harness box. The pilot was then tipped out of the seat when a small drogue parachute opened out from the top of the seat, and by means of yet another static line from the seat the parachute was deployed.

There was, however, still one more problem to overcome. It the aircraft were flying at a very high altitude and the pilot ejected, he would find himself floating down in a very rarefied atmosphere with insufficient oxygen. The result of this could be fatal, so Martin fitted to the seat a barostat which regulated the time-release mechanism. This instrument – controlled by air-pressure, which varies according to altitude – ensured that the seat and its occupant would not part company until they had descended to a height of between 13,000 and 10,000 feet.

As more and more different types of fighter and bomber aircraft were designed they presented the ejector seat designers with further problems. Aircraft like the Victor bomber and the Javelin had very high tail fins so the seats had to be altered to allow for a higher trajectory. This also gave the pilot a better chance of escape at low levels.

The problem of low-level ejection was one which grew in importance after there had been a whole series of fatal accidents involving Fleet Air Arm and R.A.F. fighter aircraft due to engine failure on take-off. There were those who refused to believe that a man could be ejected from an aircraft at runway level and live. Martin set out to prove them wrong. He cut the delay in the time release mechanism to one and a half seconds and by so doing, made the parachute open much more quickly. After a series of dummy tests, Squadron Leader John Fifield, D.F.C., A.F.C., made an ejection from a Mark 7 Meteor at Chalgrove on the 3rd September, 1955, while the aircraft was taking off. It took Fifield only six seconds to reach the ground....and he did it safely. He later went on to eject from a height of 40,000 feet, a truly remarkable achievement which was also carried out successfully.

As even faster aircraft, like the Lightnings, Phantoms and Mirages entered service, even better ejector seats were developed by Martin-Baker, the company of which James Martin was managing director. More and more lives were saved from stricken aircraft and today most of the supersonic fighter and bomber aircraft in the Western World are equipped with Martin-Baker ejector seats.

To James Martin and the intrepid Benny Lynch, along with a host of other pioneers of the ejector seat, many hundreds of pilots owe their lives. Today, pilot safety in military aircraft has reached an all-time peak with fresh improvements being continually developed as more sophisticated aircraft types come into service.

● ● ● ●

How strange the Wright Brothers would have thought both these problems and their solutions, could they have imagined them back in 1903. For them, at that time, simply to get into the air and stay there for a few seconds, at whatever risk, was enough.

This book has told the story of some of those who, like the Wright Brothers, took fantastic risks to win for man a new element through which he might move as freely as on land or sea. The story of flight is the story of those men and of countless others whose feats will never be recorded. Yet, perhaps the most astonishing fact in the adventure-packed history of aviation is that it all began only 70 years ago. A man, now eighty years old, could have stood on that beach at Kitty Hawk, as a boy of ten, and watched the whole thing begin.